Transition to retirement

A guide to inclusive practice

Roger J. Stancliffe, Nathan J. Wilson,
Nicolette Gambin, Christine Bigby and
Susan Balandin

SYDNEY UNIVERSITY PRESS

Published 2013 by Sydney University Press

SYDNEY UNIVERSITY PRESS
University of Sydney Library
sydney.edu.au/sup

© Manual – individual authors 2013
© DVD – Australian Foundation for Disability (AFFORD) 2011
© Sydney University Press 2013

Reproduction and Communication for other purposes

Except as permitted under the Act, no part of this edition may be reproduced, stored in a retrieval system, or communicated in any form or by any means without prior written permission. All requests for reproduction or communication should be made to Sydney University Press at the address below:

Sydney University Press
Fisher Library F03
University of Sydney NSW 2006 AUSTRALIA
Email: sup.info@sydney.edu.au

The forms in Appendix B may be printed or copied without prior permission by the purchaser provided that the copies are used solely by the person or organisation purchasing the original publication and appropriate acknowledgment of the source is given.

ISBN	9781743323274 (paperback)
	9781743323564 (ebook)
	9781743323731 (MOBI)

National Library of Australia Cataloguing-in-Publication entry available

Cover design by Miguel Yamin

Front cover image: Stephen composting at the community garden; back cover image: Graeme and his fellow volunteers at the community plant nursery enjoy lunch. These and other photos are provided by Australian Foundation for Disability (AFFORD) and Summer Hill Media.

Contents

Acknowledgements v
Foreword vii
Introduction ix
Abbreviations xiii

Section 1 Background 1

  1 Disability, ageing and transition to retirement 3
  2 Promoting retirement 15
  3 Laying the groundwork in the community 23

Section 2 Constructing the reality 37

  4 Planning 39
  5 Locating a group for an individual 51
  6 A new routine 61
  7 Recruiting and training mentors 77
  8 Monitoring and ongoing support 95

Section 3 Broader issues 113

  9 Conclusions 115

  Readings 129
  Appendix A Travel training 133
  Appendix B Forms 145

About the authors	155
Index	157
Transition to retirement DVD	161

Acknowledgements

The Transition to Retirement research project was supported under the Australian Research Council's Linkage Projects funding scheme (Project number: LP0989241) with the assistance of two industry partners: Australian Foundation for Disability (AFFORD) and St John of God Accord. The views expressed herein are those of the authors and are not necessarily those of the Australian Research Council or the industry partners.

AFFORD's Transition to Retirement program is partly funded by the NSW the Department of Family and Community Services, Ageing, Disability and Home Care.

The *Transition to retirement* DVD was made by AFFORD and funded by The Trust Company.

Royalties

The authors have all agreed to donate all royalties from sales of this manual to the Australian Foundation for Disability (AFFORD) to support AFFORD's Transition to Retirement program.

Foreword

As much as everyone groans from time to time about the humdrum and stresses of work, retirement is an unsettling prospect for most people. It's a major transition in anyone's life and change of this magnitude often arouses anxiety. This is much more so for people with disability, particularly intellectual disability.

Australian Disability Enterprises employ more than 20,000 people, most with intellectual and learning disabilities. It's an ageing workforce and many workers with disability are at the point in their lives when they should be considering retirement. But the lack of specialist support to assist them with the transition to retirement and the paucity of post-employment options make the prospect of retirement daunting. For many ageing workers with disability, like Kevin whose story is told in Chapter 1 of this manual, the idea of retirement signifies a loss of meaningful activity, rejection by his employer, losing his friends at work and sitting at home all day with nothing to do. It's a bleak outlook.

But, as this manual shows, it doesn't have to be like that. The Transition to Retirement (TTR) program has been developed in response to a genuine problem: the need for an effective approach to supporting older employees to build an active, socially inclusive lifestyle after retirement. The approach mapped out in this manual may not be the solution for all workers with disability, but it will certainly assist quite a few.

The TTR program emphasises social inclusion. It is consistent with the focus of the National Disability Insurance Scheme (NDIS) on building community participation and independence. It is also consistent with the National Disability Strategy's emphasis on promoting social inclusion in mainstream community settings and service systems. The TTR program supports ageing people with disability to develop new interests, skills and social networks, and facilitates their participation in mainstream community groups.

With the manual comes a DVD, which makes the idea of inclusive activities in retirement easily understandable to people with disability, their families and community organisations.

The program has grown out of collaboration between university researchers, government and a disability service provider, and is based on concerns expressed by older workers with disability and their ageing parents. The program is an evidence-based approach that has practical applications in solving a pressing problem. There should be more such collaborations. Too often university research and the needs of people with disability, their families and the disability sector are disconnected.

This TTR program manual will give practical effect to research findings and expand the horizons of people with an interest in disability service provision. It will also expand options for ageing workers with disability as they embark on a new stage of life and the disability service system moves towards the new world of the NDIS.

Ken Baker PhD
Chief Executive
National Disability Services

Introduction

This manual is based on a three-year collaborative research project, funded by the Australian Research Council (ARC), involving development and rigorous evaluation of the Transition to Retirement (TTR) program (Bigby et al., in press; Chng et al., 2012; Stancliffe, Bigby et al., 2013; Wilson et al., in press; Wilson et al., 2010). This project supported workers with long-term disability aged 45 and above to cut down a day of work and, on that free day, to join a local *mainstream* community or volunteering group of their choice.

The research articles that arose from the project are listed in the Readings section at the end of this manual. These articles provide the scientific evidence base that underpins the program that we developed in the project. As well as using research information, this manual also draws on the research team's years of service delivery experience. One of our industry partners, the Australian Foundation for Disability (AFFORD), a Sydney-based disability service provider, obtained funding to employ TTR coordinators to implement the program as part of ongoing service delivery. This enabled AFFORD to support other older workers to begin to transition to retirement, and allowed for monitoring and ongoing support (see Chapter 8) by AFFORD beyond the six-month follow-up provided for in the research project. The manual also draws on AFFORD's TTR service-delivery experience.

The Transition to retirement DVD

This manual also contains a DVD *Transition to retirement*, made by AFFORD, which includes the stories of six men and women in their 50s, 60s or 70s – Graeme, Shirley, Stephen, Laurie, Cedric and Judy – who reduced their days of work in sheltered employment and took up new enjoyable activities to prepare for retirement. These stories provide role models and give concrete examples of varied opportunities for inclusive occupation and companionship.

Transition to retirement DVD (2011)

Each person's story runs for six to eight minutes and can be viewed in full as a separate DVD chapter. Throughout this manual you will be directed to specific shorter segments of each story that illustrate key aspects of the TTR program. These segments will be identified using the DVD logo ▣, the name of the person whose story you should watch, with the start and stop times of the segment to view.

The DVD also contains other segments featuring researchers and service providers who present an overview of and commentary on the TTR program.

Introduction

People with disability

Reflecting the population of people who work in sheltered employment settings (known as Australian Disability Enterprises: ADEs), the older workers involved in the TTR project had various types of disability. These disabilities were all long term, often lifelong, and included intellectual, physical, psychiatric and sensory disabilities, as well as brain injury. Most of the participants in the project were people with lifelong intellectual disability, but some had other types of disability, including disability with a later onset, such as brain injury. Therefore, we will refer to these workers as "people with long-term disability".

Throughout the manual we recount the TTR experiences of individuals with long-term disability who took part in the TTR research project or who joined AFFORD's TTR program independent of the research. Some people preferred that we use their real name and in other cases an assumed name is used. A few stories are composites of several people's experiences. These brief stories are usually set out in a box, like Kevin's story in Chapter 1.

The purpose of this manual

This manual is intended for disability service providers and mainstream community groups. It illustrates how to implement the TTR program to achieve inclusive community participation by people with long-term disability in retirement. Older workers with long-term disability working in sheltered employment were the focus of our research and service delivery, but these ideas can also be adapted to other settings and other age groups – for example, participation in inclusive youth groups by school students with disabilities.

Abbreviations

ADEs	Australian Disability Enterprises
AFFORD	Australian Foundation for Disability
ARC	Australian Research Council
NDIS	National Disability Insurance Scheme
TTR	Transition to Retirement
WHO	World Health Organization

Section 1
Background

1
Disability, ageing and transition to retirement

People with long-term and lifelong disabilities such as Down syndrome or intellectual disability are living longer. In the late 1940s people with Down syndrome had a typical life expectancy of only 12 years. Now, people with Down syndrome have an average lifespan of 60 years. This welcome news means that many people with long-term disability are living long enough to consider retirement.

The longer life of people with disability affects disability services that provide work for them. Older workers with long-term disability make up a large and growing percentage of their workforce. Increasingly, these services need to find ways to help their older workers reduce the number of days they work and retire. Typically services do not want to simply dismiss employees who have worked with them for many years. Instead, they feel an obligation to help these workers plan for and achieve a fulfilling retirement. This manual and DVD provide detailed information about an effective approach to support older people with long-term disability start to retire. We call it the Transition to Retirement (TTR) program. This program aims to help people to gradually build an active, socially inclusive retirement lifestyle.

This chapter introduces some key retirement issues for workers with long-term disability and describes essential features of the TTR program. Later in the chapter Kevin's story illustrates the kind of support the TTR program might provide and outlines the way it would

Graeme packing boxes at work

operate. The other chapters and appendices of the manual contain more detailed information about implementing the program. The TTR program is also described in our research publications, such as Bigby et al. (in press).

> *Professor Roger Stancliffe (0:00–0:49)*
> *The need to develop a retirement lifestyle*
>
> In this clip Roger Stancliffe talks about increases in life expectancy that have occurred for many people with long-term disability, especially for individuals with intellectual disability. This means that older people with long-term disability and the disability services that support them need to find ways of reducing their hours of work

> and developing a satisfying retirement lifestyle. The TTR program provides one effective way of achieving this outcome.

Long-term disability and ageing

It is wrong to assume that all people with a long-term disability age prematurely, as most experience a pattern of ageing that is similar to other people. Although the life expectancy of people with long-term disability has increased significantly, some still have a much shorter lifespan than the general population. They include individuals with multiple disabilities or severe and profound intellectual disability. Some groups, such as people with Down syndrome, are more likely to experience the early onset of age-related conditions such as dementia. As they age, people with cerebral palsy or polio may encounter secondary health conditions associated with their disability.

The Transition to Retirement program

The main components of the TTR program are set out in Figure 1.1 together with a reference to the chapter and/or appendix containing detailed information about that component. This flow chart focuses mainly on activities directly involving a *specific individual* with long-term disability (shaded boxes). Other major elements of the program that are more broadly focused (unshaded shapes) are also included, such as promoting retirement, and laying the groundwork in the community. The dotted arrows on the left denote that, at any stage within the first 12 months, individuals with long-term disability can opt to leave the TTR program and return to their pre-existing hours of work. Of course, they are free to rejoin the TTR program at a later date.

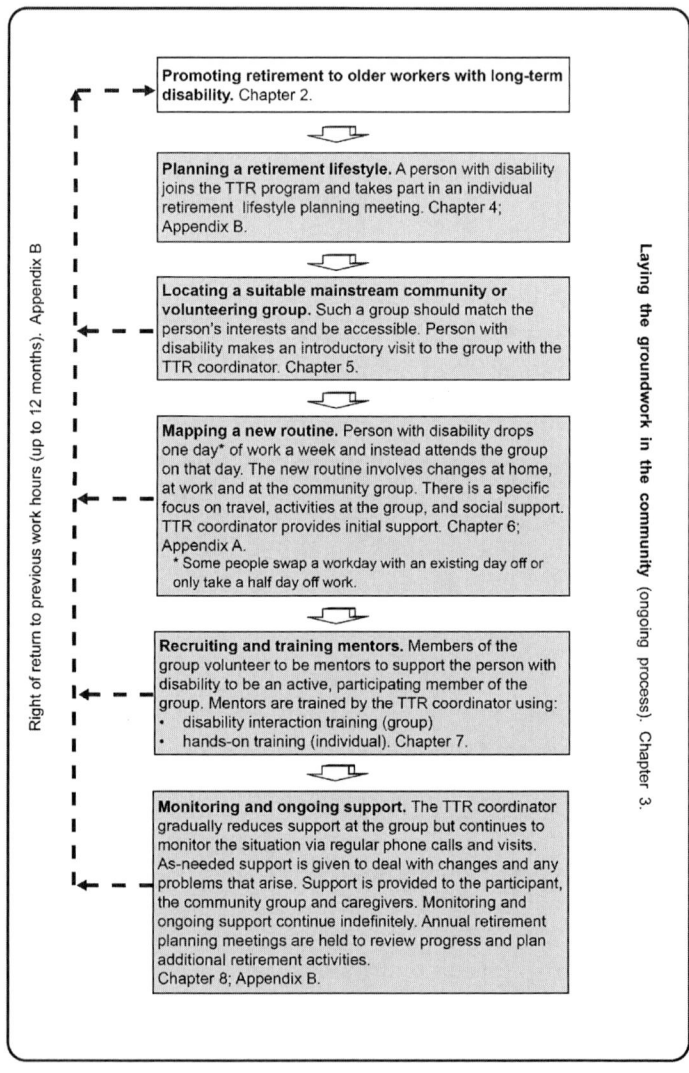

Figure 1.1 TTR program flow chart with chapter links. (Shaded boxes denote activities focussed on a specific individual with long-term disability).

> **[DVD] Professor Roger Stancliffe (0:50–1:53)**
> **Features of the Transition to Retirement program**
>
> Roger Stancliffe explains two key features of the TTR program:
>
> 1. A focus on giving people with long-term disability access to mainstream community groups and volunteering opportunities just like other retirees without disability.
> 2. The deliberate choice to support only *one* person with a long-term disability to join each community group, so that the person has that experience as an individual not as a member of a group of people with disability.

Why mainstream community groups?

The participants in this project had spent many years in disability-specific services such as sheltered employment and disability housing (e.g., group homes). People wondered if the "logical" next step following retirement from work should be a disability day service providing needed support, but with shorter hours and a more relaxed pace. Fully staffed day services are, however, expensive. Moreover, although this might suit some, this approach is not socially inclusive, and it does not reflect the typical lifestyles of other retirees without disability. At the same time, many well-established community groups already exist for the general population and for older Australians. These groups serve a wide range of different interests and needs. Why shouldn't older people with long-term disability take advantage of this existing social resource that offers an active and inclusive retirement lifestyle? If community group members are sensitised to disability issues and supported to include a person with long-term disability in their group, direct involvement of paid disability staff is minimised after the staff-intensive start-up phase (see Chapter 8). Thus, in the long run, disability service costs are likely to be lower (Wilson et al., 2010).

To allow a stable routine to be set up, we chose community groups that met at least weekly, at the same time and in the same place throughout the year. By supporting *one* person to join each group, the community group was not overwhelmed with large numbers of people with long-term disability.

Little awareness of retirement

We found that many people with long-term disability knew little about retirement and had not thought about what they would do when they stopped work. They were content to continue with their familiar routine of going to work each day and found it hard to imagine a different lifestyle. In the absence of positive role models of an active and socially connected retirement, they saw retirement as a *risky proposition* that, they worried, would result in boredom and loneliness (Bigby et al., 2011). They feared that the occupation and friendship provided at work would be lost when they retired and would not be replaced by other activities and social connections. These concerns were often shared by family members and disability service staff. Frequently, this situation meant that retirement was ignored and no planning had taken place for individuals to systematically transition from work to retirement. When a health problem or other crisis occurs that limits people's ability to work, they are utterly unprepared for this new stage of their life.

> ### *Initial views about retirement*
>
> "I've got my friends here (at work) you know I go home and I go to work that's enough for me . . . no-one thinks of retiring . . ."
> ". . . you sit at home and you don't do anything"
> *Comments by focus group participants with long-term disability.*

Kevin's story illustrates the need to actively promote retirement among older workers with long-term disability, and to provide support for these workers, their family and caregivers to start thinking about retirement. Promoting retirement is discussed in Chapter 2.

1 Disability, ageing and transition to retirement

Promoting retirement

Kevin is 57 years old. Nowadays he works only a three-day week at Sunrise Industries, a 20-minute bus trip from his group home. He has worked in this sheltered employment factory for over 25 years as a productive full-time employee. Recently, however, due to health issues (obesity, arthritis, poor physical fitness), his reduced stamina and his desire to work less, he has cut back his days of work. Even so, starting work at 8 am means he has to leave home really early. He is finding this harder and harder, and has taken more days off recently. Dianne, one of Kevin's work supervisors asks him if he has thought about retiring.

His first reaction is confusion and an unstated worry that "They are trying to get rid of me". He says to Dianne "What would I do if I didn't come to work at Sunrise? I'd just stay home with nothing to do. I wouldn't see my friends at work any more." After more discussion and reassurance that he is not going to be sacked, Dianne introduces Kevin to Sunrise's TTR coordinator, Michelle. She invites him to a lunchtime discussion about retirement.

At the meeting Michelle explains that most people do not just stop working and retire, but start by cutting down the number of days they work. She also says that it is her job to help people find enjoyable new activities and to make new friends as they move toward retirement. Michelle then shows a short DVD about an older man called Charlie. He has cut down his number of days at sheltered employment and is now enjoying being a volunteer at a local charity shop for a few hours each week on one of his non-work days.

Kevin takes home an information sheet about the TTR program. He talks to his family and his group home staff about it. His brother explains that the information sheet says that Sunrise Industries promises that he can go back to his old work schedule if things do not work out. Kevin decides that he will try the TTR program.

Limited experience of inclusive community life

These days, most disability services for adults are community based, and disability policy calls for community participation and social inclusion. Even so, many people with long-term disability have limited experience of community life, especially activities with other community members without disability. This is particularly the case for the older individuals we worked with (aged 45+ years) who grew up in an era when school inclusion was all but unknown and disability services were segregated and institutional. Typically, these older people spend their days working and living with other people with disability. When asked, they list family, other service users and disability service staff as their friends, but usually only have superficial contact with other members of their community. Importantly, most people in sheltered employment only see their work friends *at work*. This situation makes them vulnerable to social isolation and loneliness in retirement, as they are cut off from this important source of company but have few alternatives to fill this gap.

Because of their narrow experience of mainstream community life, these older workers are often unaware of the wide range of social groups and activities offered in their local communities. By contrast, workers without disabilities or with age-related disabilities frequently spend part of their time in retirement taking part in community groups, such as sporting, hobby, social or religious groups, or contributing to their community by volunteering. Through such activities they remain engaged and socially connected.

When the time comes to plan for retirement, older adults with long-term disability simply do not know what options are available and lack the skills and social connections to find out. Kevin's story continues in the box below, and we see how his retirement planning was approached.

> *Planning*
>
> Kevin, his key worker at the group home, his brother and the TTR coordinator Michelle meet over coffee and sandwiches in the lounge room at Kevin's home to talk about his transition to retirement. Be-

1 Disability, ageing and transition to retirement

fore the meeting, Michelle spent time looking around Kevin's local community, checking public transport and briefly visiting the community centre to find out about local groups.

Michelle, Kevin and his brother discuss what Kevin does on the days that he doesn't work at the moment. Kevin and his key worker explain that they do the supermarket shopping on one of these days. Otherwise, Kevin says that he "hangs around home and watches DVDs", but often feels bored. He agrees that he might be interested in trying something new. Kevin cannot say what that "something" might be. Kevin's key worker comments that recently, Kevin has been taking an interest in cooking and sometimes helps with dinner.

They all spend time talking about activities Kevin liked to do in the past – at school and when he lived with his family. His brother reminds him that, when his father was still alive, Kevin used to like working with him in the family vegetable garden.

They agree that Kevin might be interested to try activities that involve gardening or cooking. Michelle says she will look for an activity to meet one or both of these interests, but explains that it may take some time to find one. Next, they discuss practical issues that may limit the choice of activity, such as transport, suitable times and costs.

Two weeks later, Michelle contacts Kevin to say that she has found a community garden run by the local council. She explains that it is open three days per week from 10 am to 3 pm and used for growing vegetables and herbs.

A new routine

The TTR program supports each person to join a local mainstream community group that matches their interests. Once the person has tried the community group and found it to their liking, a new routine needs to be established so that participation in the group becomes a consistent part of their lifestyle. Key issues that need to be dealt with include:

- travel to and from the group

- costs of membership and any weekly fees
- activities while at the group
- support for participation in activities and social interaction within the group
- troubleshooting and back-up support when things go wrong or change.

In the TTR program, long-term support within the group is given by the group members who volunteer to be mentors. Mentors are given training and support by the TTR coordinator. These issues are explored in depth in Chapters 6 and 7. Travel training is examined in Appendix A.

Let's continue Kevin's story to gain a picture of how this all can work.

A new routine

Kevin and Michelle decide that Tuesday is a good day to take off from work and go to the community garden. Michelle organised the visit by speaking to the community garden group leader. Michelle found out that Kevin could catch the bus to the garden, but initially she drives him and stays the whole time. Although anxious and shy at first, by the third visit Kevin feels more relaxed about talking to the other people in the group and gardening alongside them. On the way home, he tells Michelle that he wants to keep on going to the garden on Tuesdays.

For the next five weeks, each Tuesday Michelle teaches Kevin to travel safely to and from the garden by bus. It is the same bus that he catches to work, but he gets off five stops closer to home. There is then a 10–15-minute walk to the garden.

Kevin now enjoys sleeping in on Tuesdays. He arrives at the garden about 10.30 am and stays till 2.45 pm when he leaves to catch the bus home. He works on tasks such as watering, weeding and mulching, but needs guidance about what to do and when to do it. Everyone has morning tea and lunch as a group in the meeting room and Kevin joins in.

1 Disability, ageing and transition to retirement

Two gardeners who come regularly on Tuesdays, Seeta and Frank, seem to enjoy showing Kevin how to do different gardening tasks. Michelle talks to each of them about helping Kevin and being his "mentors". Michelle explains that this means showing Kevin how to do different gardening tasks, reminding him what needs to be done, sometimes working alongside him, introducing him to other gardeners, and quietly reminding him of "unwritten" group rules such as remembering to bring biscuits for morning tea when it is his turn. Over the coming weeks Michelle provides training, guidance and advice to the mentors as they learn how they can best support Kevin's participation in the group. Seeta suggests that Kevin takes on the responsibility for delivering wheelbarrow loads of mulch to other gardeners. Kevin agrees and Seeta shows him what to do. Quite soon this role becomes recognised as "Kevin's job" and other gardeners call on Kevin to bring them mulch.

Some weeks Kevin is proud to take home vegetables and herbs grown at the garden. At home he is supported to cook using them.

There is no cost to come to the garden. People bring their own lunch and take turns in bringing snacks for morning tea. This means that even though Kevin is earning less now because he has dropped a day of work, the cost is easily affordable on his disability pension.

Kevin enjoys gardening each week and gets to know the people there. He does not see them at other times except for bumping into Seeta at the shopping centre now and then. In December, he goes to the community garden Christmas party at a local club. Kevin's mentor Frank says that he also goes to the garden on Fridays and that Kevin should think about coming on Fridays as well.

Participants' comments after six months going to their community group

"I'll keep on doing it for the rest of my life." (Lawn bowls)
"People are so nice . . . We talk about all sorts of things." (Seniors' social group)

> "They're my mates ... they look after me, they talk to me ... and sometimes I help them." (Men's Shed)

Monitoring and ongoing support

Many adults with long-term disability continue to go to their community group long term and it becomes part of their lifestyle. As they become more comfortable and familiar with the group, and a stable routine is set up, their support needs may diminish. As well, mentors become better at providing effective support and suitable activities. These factors mean that, over time, the TTR coordinator can reduce day-to-day involvement. However, when group activities alter, mentors move on, or the person's needs change, renewed short-term support from the TTR coordinator is often needed to deal with these issues. This means that ongoing light-touch monitoring and as-needed support remain necessary indefinitely. These matters are examined thoroughly in Chapter 8.

2
Promoting retirement

Retirement is a relatively new concept for many people with long-term disability. Although many older people with long-term disability leave work, it is often due to a crisis such as a health problem or changed family circumstances rather than because they want to retire. This means that the idea of planning for retirement needs to be positively promoted to people with long-term disability. Questions that people may have include: What is retirement? What do you do in retirement? How do you keep contact with friends in retirement? How will retirement affect your income?

This chapter provides detailed information about how to embed the concept of retirement into the everyday experience of people with long-term disability, their families, disability staff and caregivers.

What messages about retirement are important?

Retirement seminars and superannuation information sessions are a regular occurrence in most workplaces. Workers without long-term disability usually plan and look forward to a retirement that involves swapping work for a range of meaningful pursuits. Mainstream policy makers refer to this concept as *active ageing*. The World Health Organization (WHO) states that active ageing is the process where individuals participate in society as they age and experience the health, social and

Stephen: 40 years of work and still working!

wellbeing benefits that come from meaningful participation (WHO, 2002).

So, what are the key themes that can be drawn from the WHO policy?

1. Ageing should be about continued participation in society.
2. Individuals should be supported to realise their potential as they age.
3. Meaningful participation offers many personal and social benefits.

2 Promoting retirement

For people with long-term disability, who often have experienced a lifetime of exclusion, such ideals may appear unattainable. Unlike most retirees, people with long-term disability can rarely base their future retirement lifestyles upon concrete role models of peers enjoying these ideals. In our research, we learnt that people with long-term disability often saw retirement as a "risky" idea (Bigby et al., 2011). In Chapter 1, Kevin's story shows how he was anxious about what he would do if he didn't go to work and see his friends there. That is, work plays an important and enjoyable role in the lives of many people with long-term disability, providing both activity and social connections. Consequently, any change may be faced with concern.

 Cedric (0:36–1:57)

Retirement concepts

This scene shows Cedric's niece Sue talking about Cedric's enjoyment of work, how she broached the idea of retirement with him and his preconceived ideas about what retirement meant.

How can we support people with long-term disability to understand that, with support, the ideals of active ageing are more than achievable for them and that leaving work is not something to fear?

Delivering positive messages about ageing and retirement

Listed below are steps that can be taken, either singly or together, to make transition to retirement an everyday reality for people with long-term disability. Just as superannuation information sessions are the norm in many workplaces, discussions about retirement with workers with long-term disability could also become the norm!

Create an older workers group

It is common for high school students with and without long-term disability to visit a workplace for work experience. It is common for new school leavers with long-term disability to join the workplace as part of a transition to work program. These activities are normative processes that are well understood and accepted as part of the lifecycle. A 45+ group for people with long-term disability could be based on the same premise – a subgroup of workers who are united by their age. For example, scheduling a monthly BBQ could provide older workers with disability with opportunities to talk and learn about issues related to ageing and retirement in an informal setting.

 Tip

Set up an annual program of activities including guest speakers, videos, small discussion groups, a Christmas party and acknowledging birthdays for the month. Such activities celebrate ageing and could assist workers to start planning and thinking about their transition to retirement.

Develop a regular and accessible newsletter

Good quality newsletters are a great source of information, particularly if written in an accessible style and complemented by informative images. They are a perfect way to give concrete examples of older people with long-term disability developing a retirement lifestyle. The use of large print, simple English and clearly illustrated text assists people with reading problems to understand the content. Newsletters are also easily placed on websites and mailed via email lists and so can be accessed by a range of key stakeholders.

Recruit some well-respected flag bearers to spread the word

Within each work setting there are characters who are well liked and well respected by their peers. When one of these in-house leaders has started their transition to retirement journey, they could be invited to act as a flag-bearer. For example, Laurie and Graeme featured in the DVD have supported the research team by giving presentations about their new non-work activities – singing in a community choir and volunteering at a community plant nursery – at conferences, self-advocacy groups, lectures and in-house presentations at their workplaces.

These activities are a real highlight and get folk talking about retirement. This method presents a positive retirement message from respected peers – "If Graeme can do that, maybe I can too."

Hold information sessions for families and caregivers

Every disability service has functions each year where families and caregivers meet. These opportunities present the perfect occasion to showcase some positive transition to retirement stories such as those in the accompanying DVD. It is important to make sure that two key messages are presented to families and caregivers:

1. that retirement should be a positive stage of life
2. that the TTR program is one evidence-based program that suits many, but perhaps not all people.

Once you gain a caregiver's attention at such an event, there is a chance that a more personalised discussion will follow. This could include the need for more detail about what the program might mean for an individual so that a personalised decision could be made. In turn, this could lead to individual retirement planning which is discussed in detail in Chapter 4.

Embedding retirement into everyday reality for disability service staff

Disability service staff are often the greatest champions for people with long-term disability, but because of their key role they can also inadvertently be a barrier to person-centred outcomes. So, strategies are also needed that encourage staff to become "true believers" in supporting transition to retirement.

Retirement education: not stopping work totally, just changing the balance

Some disability employment service managers and staff may see participation in mainstream community groups as too difficult for their employees with long-term disability. Likewise, they may feel that the employees' social and vocational needs are currently being met at work. So, educating disability service staff to think beyond the person's current work situation and consider future needs in retirement is as important as educating everybody else.

Staff education sessions about a new TTR program need to be embedded into the annual staff training calendar. These sessions should provide education on retirement indicators, what the program offers, how the program works, how to access the program and how to embed the program into the annual individual person-centred planning process.

Embedding retirement into policy and service planning forms

Significant change cannot be sustained without formally embedding new processes into policy and procedures. However, there are many issues to consider before making changes to policy and practice to avoid negative unintended consequences. For example, at what age can a person start in a TTR program – if it is as young as 45 years how might this affect the overall demographic of the workplace? Should eligibility be less about age, but more about retirement indicators such as declining health, reduced wellbeing, absenteeism, disengagement at work and falls in individual productivity?

Appendix B contains an individualised retirement lifestyle planning form (for the first retirement planning meeting), and an annual retirement lifestyle planning review form (for annual review meetings), that can be used for TTR planning. These forms can be embedded into the individual planning and review cycles of disability services.

A gradual reduction in days at work

> Having control in the timing and manner of leaving work had a positive impact on psychological and social wellbeing. (De Vaus et al., 2007, p. 679)

It is very important that employees with long-term disability (and their families) feel in control of the pace and timing of their transition to retirement (Stancliffe, Wilson et al., 2013). Mainstream retirement research tells us that such control is associated with better health and social outcomes in retirement.

Therefore, a good way to introduce a TTR program is to make it a gradual process – where an employee progresses from full-time to part-time work, reducing hours over time. This approach means that most of the employee's existing work-related social ties and routines are maintained while at the same time he/she is developing new non-work activities that can be continued into retirement. Quite often we noticed that once employees had dropped a day at work, and enjoyed the more relaxed schedule of going to their community group, their energy levels increased. Furthermore, their retirement indicators, such as absence rates decreased and their productivity at work increased. However, disability employment services wanting to use this approach need to enable a gradual reduction in work hours.

Right of return

One of our most successful start-up strategies was providing a right of return letter. This meant that participants could try transition to retirement BUT were safe in the knowledge that if retirement did not work out, they could return to their pre-existing work arrangements. This helped them to feel in control of the process (Stancliffe, Wilson et al., 2013). The letter provided strong reassurance that the employee had nothing to lose. It also helped neutralise the unstated fear that the real aim of the transition was to "get rid of" the employee. Even though this fear was unfounded, it was nevertheless real for some older employees and so had to be dealt with. Appendix B provides an example of a right of return letter – an effective guarantee at a time of significant change.

> **DVD** *Laurie (0:41–1:11)*
> _Right of return_
>
> Laurie describes how he wanted to join a singing group in retirement. He explains that he was given the option of returning to work if he didn't like it.

Retirement indicators

The approaches to promoting retirement described in this chapter should be widely available so people can self-select into a TTR program. However, some individuals may not recognise that reduced work hours or retirement could be beneficial to them. They may need a specific invitation and encouragement to take the first step toward retirement. Identifying people who could benefit from a TTR program involves considering the following indicators:

- health problems and frequent absences from work due to illness
- slowing down with reduced productivity at work
- often being late to work because of problems with getting up early enough
- no longer enjoying some or many aspects of work
- social withdrawal at work or avoiding work tasks (e.g., sleeping)
- excessive tiredness or irritability.

A first step is to discuss these issues with the person and other important individuals in their life. The presence of these indicators may not always mean that retirement is the best option. Changing work tasks, treating health problems or getting more rest may be more appropriate responses in some cases.

3
Laying the groundwork in the community

Just as people with long-term disability often have little experience participating in mainstream community groups, so too people without disability have limited opportunities to meet or talk with people with long-term disability. Therefore, one of the primary roles of the TTR coordinator is to bridge the gap between mainstream community groups and people with disability. However, acting as a bridge is quite a skilled task and one that, if not done well, can take a long time to restore. A lot of time is devoted to laying the groundwork with community groups when first setting up a TTR program. This task also needs to be given ongoing attention, with the TTR coordinator making contact with new groups and maintaining a relationship with familiar groups, even when there is no person with long-term disability currently attending the group.

This chapter provides an overview of the key tasks required to lay the groundwork for supporting people with long-term disability to participate in their community. The chapter includes clarification of the distinction between volunteering and community groups, guidelines on how to find appropriate volunteering and community groups, and suggestions for judging the general suitability of a group to include a member with long-term disability. Information about locating a suitable group for a specific person with particular interests is presented in Chapter 5.

Jeff – an integral member of the Men's Shed community

A range of community groups

Each and every community has a network of community groups, associations, clubs and volunteering services. These groups cater for people of different ages, but there are invariably a number of groups for older and retired people who have more time on their hands. Knowing where these groups are and how to access them can be difficult for people with long-term disability, hence the need for support from the TTR coordinator.

Volunteering

Volunteering means giving your time to help other people or to help in your community. People volunteer for many different reasons – to meet new people, to learn new skills, to try something new, and to "give back" to their community. Usually people will choose to volunteer for a group that means something to them. Alternatively, people may volunteer because a group offers a certain activity or a set of skills that

3 Laying the groundwork in the community

appeal to the person, such as helping out with a community garden. In the DVD Shirley joined the Cat Protection Society because she wanted to help animals.

Every community is likely to have a local agency that can support people who want to volunteer to find a suitable opportunity. Larger organisations like Volunteer Australia provide advocacy and a policy focus on the volunteering process across Australia – their website provides information about a range of volunteering opportunities available: www.govolunteer.com.au.

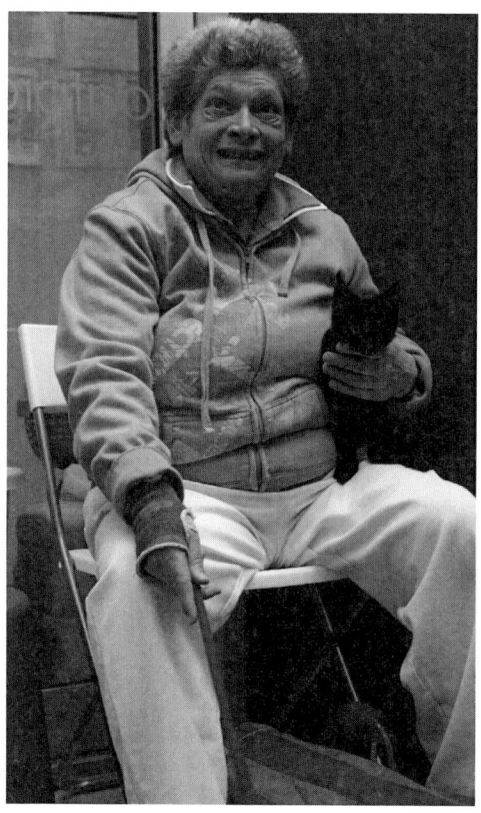

Shirley with a kitten

One key difference between voluntary work and paid work is that the volunteer generally decides which activities to join and for how long. Unlike employment, there is no requirement for volunteers to be "working" constantly, in other words it is okay to chat or chill out on the job, and the "boss" does not have the right to insist that a volunteer performs a job that he/she does not like doing. Volunteers do have a responsibility to complete the tasks they have chosen, but have the freedom to do only those tasks that they select.

In Australia, people who volunteer for an average of eight hours per week may qualify to keep the "mobility allowance"[1] – a government supplement to the disability support pension to help meet the costs of travelling to work or voluntary work. This allowance is worth more than $40 per week, so losing this income after stopping work can be a strong reason for people not wanting to retire. Volunteering in retirement can enable individuals to retain the mobility allowance.

Volunteering can be a good choice for people who:

- have a special interest in the types of activities that involve volunteering (e.g., restoring aircraft)
- want to contribute to their community (e.g., working in a charity store or community soup kitchen)
- would find the loss of government benefits, such as the mobility allowance, difficult financially.

Here are some examples of volunteering opportunities that TTR participants joined during the research project.

Community (soup) kitchen	Cat protection society *#
Community nursery *	Charity store *#
Aviation museum #	Frail-aged social group

these groups are shown in the stories on the DVD
 # this group's members were all of the same sex

---

1 Eligibility for the mobility allowance is subject to change. Readers should check current eligibility details and payment amounts with Centrelink at www.humanservices.gov.au/customer/themes/people-with-a-disability.

3 Laying the groundwork in the community

Community groups

Most communities will have a seniors' centre or a neighbourhood/civic centre that has a range of programs and groups that use the facility. In Australia, the grassroots phenomenon of community-based Men's Sheds represents a group that is gender-specific.

Community groups take a variety of organisational forms. These range from formal, funded groups with some paid staff (e.g., a local government seniors' centre), to established groups with their own building run by a committee (e.g., a Men's Shed), to very informal groups of individuals with a shared interest and consensus-based leadership arrangements (e.g., a knitting group that meets in a local community hall).

There is an amazing range of community groups – you name it, there is likely to be a group to celebrate that activity or hobby! Each urban community will have a range of sporting, social, craft, exercise, hobby and garden groups. In our research study people joined a wide variety of community groups.

Men's Shed #	Community garden *
Seniors' group *	Exercise # and social group
Seniors choir *	Community (teaching) kitchen
Lawn bowls club	Seniors' art group *
Seniors 10-pin bowling league	Walking and knitting group

* these groups are shown in the stories on the DVD
# this group's members were all of the same sex

One of the great things about all of the community groups that we worked with was that they almost always offered MORE than just the stated aim of the group. For example, here are details about two different and diverse community groups:

Seniors' choir – for older people who love to sing, but as the choir was attached to the local seniors' centre, after an hour of singing with friends, there was a shared morning tea followed by a larger group meeting and social events such as a guest presenter.

Seniors' art group – for older people with a liking for art, held at the local activity centre. Morning tea occurred prior to art and was followed by lunch, and then a seniors exercise class for those interested.

A community group can be a good choice for people who:

- are particularly interested in the type of activity the group deals with (e.g., community choir, exercise group)
- have a certain range of skills that are well matched to the group's activities
- are very sociable and want to meet new people
- are adaptable to change and the often busy nature of larger groups.

Finding community groups

Some groups are high profile and so are easy to track down; they may even have their own building with a sign on the front such as the Cat Protection Society's cattery and charity shop (see Shirley's story on the DVD). Other groups are small and very informal, so may only be known to members and friends. For example, a craft group that gets together in a meeting room at the local library.

Strategies you can use to find these different types of community groups include:

- asking older people (or people who have an older relative) who live in the local area
- subscribing to seniors' newsletters
- keeping an eye on the community sections of local newspapers
- visiting, in person or online, local government information services, community centres and local public libraries.

In the TTR research project, we had little success in gaining information about nearby mainstream community groups from the local disability services that our participants used. This may reflect these services' primary focus on disability-specific settings.

3 Laying the groundwork in the community

First contact

There are a number of ways to make the first contact, but first you need to present yourself as a non-threatening advocate for people with long-term disability. A key point to remember is that these community groups have existed, often for many years, within the community and their membership usually operates within a set of formal and unwritten rules that are often specific to the group. Also, many of the members have worked all of their life and are involved in the group for their own personal enjoyment and wellbeing – any perceived threat to that peaceful and stable reality will usually be met with some concern. Typically, when making an initial contact with a group, you would start by talking to the leader or coordinator of the group.

A non-threatening advocate

Before you knock on any doors, it is important to consider what messages you are going to give and to acknowledge that many myths and stereotypes about people with long-term disability exist in mainstream society. That is, group members may think that all people with long-term disability can be aggressive, or overly cuddly, or that all people with disability have epilepsy and could have a seizure.

Firstly, ask yourself the following questions:

- How are you going to dress and present yourself?
- Why are you knocking on the door?
- What are you going to say to the person who answers the door?
- What impression are you going to leave with the group?

The bigger picture that you want to convey is that there is a group of fellow citizens who, like the members of the group, are at the end of their working life and want to do something more than sit at home and watch TV. The difference is that these citizens have long-term disability and that they need some help to achieve the same goals as the regular members. That is, you are emphasising that the person with disability and the group members have a lot in common, and you are appealing to the group's sense of fairness to reach out to this person who is missing out.

Often, members of groups that cater for seniors already have experience of disability. Because the incidence of disability increases with age, there may be some group members with mobility limitations, or others who have difficulty with speech after a stroke. However, these disabilities usually occur after many decades of life without disability. By contrast, the participants in the TTR project had lived all or most of their life with disability, typically including decades spent working and living in settings for people with long-term disability.

Here are some tips on how to make a first approach to a community group:

- Don't go dressed in a suit and tie, but also don't dress in weekend clothing such as what you might wear to the beach. Just dress in smart casual clothes with a neat shirt or blouse. This style of clothing will be suitable for just about all group types and will convey a positive and respectful image to the group's members.
- You are knocking on the door as an interested and inquisitive advocate for a group of older citizens with long-term disability. That is, you are not there to "sell" a product or to convince the community group members to do something that they do not wish to do. Likewise you are not there to press them about any obligation to fulfil the charter of rights for people with disability. Rather, you are trying to find common ground between the interests and circumstances of group members and the person with disability you are supporting. This means you should ask about group members and their backgrounds.
- There are four main messages you will want to get across – 1) introduce yourself professionally, for example, as "Mary Smith from Sunrise Disability Services". 2) Ask for the group leader and inform him/her that you are a professional working with local older people with disability. Name the person, if you have a person in mind, to personalise the situation. 3) Advise that you are hoping to help people with long-term disability identify what kinds of opportunities *might* exist in the community to help with a gradual transition to retirement. 4) Invite the group leader to share more formal information with you about the group such as activities, operating days, hours, costs and membership criteria.

- The impression you want to leave is that *if* you came back with a person who has a long-term disability that group members would look forward to seeing you again and would be interested in meeting the person with disability. You want to make it clear that you are not trying to hijack their group by imposing a large group of people with disability who have nowhere else to go.

Supporting the person with disability to make the first visit(s) to the group is described in Chapter 6.

Getting to know the key leaders and key stakeholders

Many of the members of different community groups know each other and many attend more than one group each week – this is active ageing! Therefore, it is important to recognise that the impression you give at one group will be relayed quickly to the next. Of course this can work in a positive way and make it easier to introduce yourself to a different but related group. It is important to gain an idea of who is who within each community – who are the leaders and who are the key stakeholders – and gradually to be included in these networks.

As you get to know these key stakeholders, chances are they will start inviting you to their annual Christmas party or to participate in a community forum about ageing. For example, during the TTR research project, the local seniors group asked us to give a presentation at one of their weekly meetings – when we did this they were fascinated about the research process and how applied research worked. We did not fit their stereotype of researchers wearing their lab coats and looking down microscopes! Another example was Graeme who was supported to volunteer at a local community plant nursery – some time later the council (i.e., the local government body for the city) also opened a community garden on the same site with a pizza oven for a men's cooking group. We were invited along to the launch; attending these activities is vital to building and sustaining community partnerships.

Establishing trust and building relationships

This is perhaps the most critical point and is affected by all that you do. Trust can be fragile. It can take many weeks to build up trust, and one

Graeme at the community garden launch

day to destroy it. A cautionary example involved members of a community Men's Shed who, when approached by us, told us the story of a local disability service arriving with a busload of men expecting that the men at the shed would open the doors to "look after" the men with disability. As it turned out the men at the shed were most annoyed that their group had been treated with such disrespect and that the men with disability were being "fobbed off" onto a group of unknown men.

3 Laying the groundwork in the community

Trust and relationships are central to breaking down disabling barriers. As we will see in later chapters, it is essential for group members to get to know the person with disability *as an individual* who has interests and a personal identity, rather than being just a representative of some impersonal larger group of people with disability.

Similarly, trust and relationships are not readily transferrable from one TTR coordinator to the next. Wherever possible, a single coordinator should handle all contact with a particular community group. There definitely should not be a faceless passing parade of disability workers who interact with group members. Consistent personal contact reinforces trust and makes communication easier and more informal.

 Tip

When it is necessary to involve another coordinator, this should be done by personal face-to-face introduction, and with the recognition that the new coordinator will need to build his or her own relationships.

What makes a suitable group?

For the TTR project we had some criteria that each group usually needed to meet before we considered introducing a person to that group. Most important was that the group met *year round* (excluding a typical break at Christmas), that it met on the *same day at the same time and at the same location*, that the group *met for at least two hours*, and that the group was *affordable* for a person on the disability support pension. These are important, straightforward criteria to ensure that, should a person with disability join the group, a new, predictable and affordable routine can easily be established (see Chapter 6).

> **Joanne joins a knitting group: second time lucky!**
>
> One example that did not work so well involved Joanne who wanted to join a knitting group. A local knitting group was found that met all the criteria mentioned above, except that no-one told us that they only met during the winter months. This group worked a treat for the first few weeks until we found out that the group would cease meeting within the next month for an eight-month summer recess. So we needed to find another group for Joanne, and quickly! Luckily we were able to find Joanne a new knitting group whose members also took part in a walking group beforehand – another of Joanne's interests!

We also limited our focus to groups that gathered on weekdays during the day, so that the person's new activity replaced a day of work wherever possible. Meeting at these times is quite common among community groups that have a number of retirees as members. However, groups also operate at other times of day and on the weekend. Thus there is a range of opportunities that can form part of an inclusive, active retirement lifestyle. Indeed, one of our participants, Laurie, has been supported to use his public transport skills to travel on Saturdays to a lawn bowling club located a few blocks away from where he sings in the community choir on a weekday (see Laurie's story on the DVD).

What if the group just does not feel right?

Another key factor is whether or not the group and its members appear to embrace the idea of a person with long-term disability joining their group. Often they articulate this in a matter-of-fact way such as "anyone can join our group – the more the merrier". By contrast, there are groups that just don't feel right. It may not be anything the group members say or do, it may just not feel like it has the potential to be a supportive and inclusive environment for people with long-term disability. In this case it is often better to drop by a second time and if you have the same feeling, then it is usually not worth pursuing this particular group.

3 Laying the groundwork in the community

Overwhelmingly, groups were very welcoming, but in a small number of instances issues arose. In some cases, the activities or members of the group were not a good fit with the person's interests or support needs. For example, one activity group made it very clear that any members had to be fully mobile with no additional support needs. This meant that any request to provide even the smallest amount of support would not "fit" with the group's entry criteria.

Joanne at the new knitting group

In other cases, practical issues intervened that made the situation unsuitable. For example, a volunteering opportunity at a popular museum was not viable because there was a very long waiting list of people wanting to volunteer.

In a few instances, the group claimed to welcome people with long-term disability, but identified barrier after barrier – issues such as eligibility, safety and an alleged lack of opportunities and activities. As soon as one issue was dealt with another arose, and we soon reached the conclusion that the group was not appropriate at this time. Nevertheless, it might be a group that the TTR program could work with in the longer term to develop members' confidence and capacity to include a person with disability.

The next chapter will focus on individual planning. This is followed by a detailed insight in Chapter 5 into finding a community group *for an individual*.

Section 2
Constructing the reality

4
Planning

Good planning lies at the heart of person-centred action. We know that any change in a person's life can be difficult, disruptive and emotionally draining. Therefore, the planning stage of the TTR program is perhaps *the* most crucial to get right and do well. This chapter provides a step-by-step summary of how we implemented person-centred retirement lifestyle planning in the TTR project.

The elephant in the room – older age!

Before you hold a retirement planning meeting, the first thing to do is to meet the person informally. Have a chat about getting older and why the TTR program might be worth considering. This conversation may help people with long-term disability understand and consider that as we age we enter a different life stage and may need to start thinking about making changes in our lives. It is important to have this conversation and reach an agreement that the person with disability may be interested in trying out the TTR program before any planning meeting, as you need the person's permission to hold a meeting.

The planning meeting could be presented as follows: "Let's get together with some important people in your life to talk about getting older and what this means for you". One outcome of the planning meeting may be an agreement that the person will start the transition to retirement journey, but it is an equally valid outcome if the person decides to continue working.

Sometimes this first meeting may not lead anywhere immediately but a seed will have been sown. For example, in the TTR project we met with Doug and his mother to talk about getting older. Doug was keen to try the TTR program, but his family felt that it was a little bit too early for him as he was only 45. About 12 months later, the family contacted us and suggested we meet as they now felt that it was a good time to talk about Doug trialling the program. Importantly, you are putting the power in the hands of the person with disability and the family, power that they are often denied by rigid services and funding structures. Be-

Doug is now a keen bowler and part-time worker

ing in control of your retirement contributes to better post-retirement outcomes.

> ### Jeff's story
>
> Jeff had been working at the factory since he was in his early 20s. Jeff is now 60 and because of deteriorating mobility has been struggling to maintain working four days per week. Recently his sister was confronted with his diminishing health and reduced productivity and so agreed to the disability service provider's suggestion that Jeff cut back to three days per week. When the TTR program was announced Jeff showed an interest, but he said he needed to talk to his sister about anything like this first. We arranged a time to meet and Jeff's sister was relieved that someone wanted to talk about ageing and what Jeff might do as he grew older. So, this informal meeting was not a planning meeting, but just a discussion about the key issues to do with Jeff as he was ageing. We learnt that change had always been difficult for Jeff and his sister, and that looming change due to retirement was causing great anxiety. Jeff and everyone agreed that trying the TTR program was good idea and so we arranged to meet again to plan.

Before the planning meeting

An important preparatory step is to find out about the abilities and support needs of the person with long-term disability, and to chat informally with the person at his/her workplace. This will give you both a chance to get to know each other a little better and will mean that when the planning meeting occurs, the ice will have already been broken. Often you also meet the person's colleagues and may learn a lot about the context of the person's life and the role that work plays in it. Informal conversations over a cup of coffee at morning tea can often teach you more than you will ever learn at a formal meeting where an individual may feel anxious or not confident enough to say much. This meeting at work also has a positive spin-off in that other workers will get to know you and will associate you with supporting their peers to do something exciting as they grow older. When the time comes to begin a retirement conversation with these peers you will already have created a positive set of expectations about the transition process!

Before the planning meeting it is always best to be prepared with as much detailed knowledge about the person's local area as possible. This includes details such as where the person lives, where the nearest public transport stops are, the details of the local community transport scheme, what range of groups are present in the immediate area, and what is available in a slightly wider area.

You also need to be prepared and have some insight into how flexible the person's disability employment service is willing to be in case working days or hours need to be changed. Sometimes you might find what seems to be the perfect local group, but if the day that the group meets is on a current working day that cannot be altered, this may not work out. Building a good relationship with key personnel at all levels of service delivery can lead to rules being bent to accommodate an individual who is trying something new.

 Dr Nathan Wilson (2:49–3:33)

Planning a gradual transition to retirement

Nathan Wilson explains that retirement planning may not be difficult for family members and the person with disability because the planning is not crisis driven, and the transition from work to retirement is gradual with the person with disability in control of the pace and extent of change.

The retirement lifestyle planning meeting – past, present and the future

Step 1 – Book the meeting

In the TTR project we ran the retirement lifestyle planning meeting in a very informal way in a setting where the person with disability was comfortable. If possible and if the person agrees, it is always good to try

4 Planning

and include family as well as disability service representatives, such as a key worker.

Step 2 – Start the meeting

A good way to start these kinds of meetings is to mix any introductions with some light-hearted banter about how we are all getting older and that it is great for all of us to make plans for the day when we might think about reducing our days at work. Often in our study, each participant talked about how old they were and what life-stage they were currently facing.

 Tip

Serving drinks and snacks can reduce the formality of the situation and help people feel more relaxed. These refreshments can be brought out at the start or later in the meeting when a break is needed.

Stephen's planning meeting – a relaxed chat in the lounge room over a cup of coffee

Step 3 – Talk about the past

Talking about the past is a great way to begin a reflection on what the person has done and enjoyed during his/her life. This is a chance for the person with disability and family members to recall childhood memories and other experiences when younger and the types of activities and hobbies that the person used to take part in. This reflection is important as it often yields valuable information about the person's interests that the group members might not think to tell you.

> *Jeff's planning meeting – his past informs his future*
>
> At Jeff's planning meeting all that we could discover was that Jeff really liked sport. Beyond watching TV sport for hours he had never actually played any sport, so could not really say what it was that he liked about sport and what it was that he might like to try. When focussing on Jeff's teenage years when his physical disability was not as severe, we learnt that he would cycle all over the place. He spent hours tinkering with his bike – pulling the gears apart, putting them back together, oiling the chain, and so on. This gave us an insight that led Jeff to join a Men's Shed where tinkering with such mechanical items was one part of a wider suite of activities. Jeff loves the Men's Shed, has cut down his days at work, and still enjoys watching sport on TV.

Step 4 – Talk about the present

Having spent some time discussing the past and using this as time for reminiscences, the focus needs to be brought back to the present. There are several key tasks that can be divided into two broad objectives: mapping the person's current interests and hobbies, and discussing in as much detail as possible the person's current functional skills and support needs. For the TTR project we developed a Retirement Lifestyle Planning form – see Appendix B. This form helps guide discussion on these two key issues.

Mapping the person's existing interests and hobbies is quite uncomplicated as they are current and there should be a fair bit to talk

4 Planning

Jeff at the Men's Shed

about. For example, Laurie is renowned as a singer, so at his planning meeting there was a lot of discussion about his singing, what music he liked, what radio station he listened to, and what his favourite songs were.

> **DVD** *Shirley (4:57–7:11)*
> *Retirement planning meeting*
>
> These scenes show the TTR coordinator meeting with Shirley at home for her retirement lifestyle planning meeting. Her house staff also attend and together they discuss Shirley's interests and what concerns they have about the program. The TTR coordinator is flexible about the approach in order for Shirley to participate comfortably in the program.

The person's functional skills and support needs are usually straightforward to understand, as they too are current. Functional skills to focus on include money management, travel, communication and telephone skills. Important support needs to discuss include medication, health and health needs (e.g. epilepsy, any dietary issues), behaviour and self-care needs.

Narelle's skills and support needs

At Narelle's planning meeting we learnt that she needs help with many areas of daily life and her limited communication means that she needs support whenever she is out in the community. We also learnt that she had no health problems and great self-care skills meaning that she needed no support with medication or self-care. This meant any community group and new routine for Narelle needed to ensure that her skill limitations (e.g., understanding of road safety) would not place her at any risk of harm. We found a local seniors' group for Narelle that provided transport, was in a well-appointed but safely contained building, and had existing structures for collection of money and provided a hot cooked lunch.

Step 5 – Talk about the future

This is often the most difficult part of the planning meeting as so few people with disability, like many employees without disability have

4 Planning

Narelle at her seniors' group

made any concrete plans for the future. This part of the meeting can be started with the statement "imagine you are retired and didn't go to work anymore . . . what would you do?"

Quite often the answer is "I don't know, I haven't thought about that yet."

The next step is to progress the conversation toward thinking about "practising" retirement by having a go at the TTR program.

To do this, you need to offer ideas about what types of possibilities there are in the local community and to give an overview of what other people in the program have become involved in. It is most important to clarify that the TTR program is about *replacing* one day at work by either doing some volunteer work, or by joining a community group.

These ideas need concrete examples and clear explanation such as "volunteering means helping other people or helping out in your community". The individual stories on the *Transition to retirement* DVD can be helpful in providing specific examples.

> *Peter helps out at the bookstore*
>
> At Peter's lifestyle planning meeting we learnt that he already took part in some social activities and games nights within the residential complex where he lived. He seemed to like the idea of "helping out" and so this meant that volunteering was more likely to be a good choice for him, even though he couldn't really tell us what kind of volunteering he wanted to do. We found that a local charity had set up a second-hand bookstore that was run by volunteers. Peter seemed interested and started volunteering once he had tried it out for a few hours. Three years later Peter is still busy at the bookstore, but now he volunteers twice a week!

Step 6 – Agree on outcomes and what the next steps will be

It is vital to leave the meeting with a clear agenda about who is going to do what and when the next meeting will be. The TTR coordinator needs to take on the bulk of the responsibility in this situation. This includes the key task of finding a potentially suitable community group or volunteering opportunity for the person to try. Chapter 5 describes the process of finding a group for a specific individual and evaluating to what degree it matches with the person with disability's interests and needs.

4 Planning

Peter tidying the magazine shelf

5
Locating a group for an individual

In Chapter 3 we outlined how to familiarise yourself with local community groups and volunteering opportunities, as well as how to judge the general suitability of these groups to include a member with long-term disability. In this chapter we examine the task of successfully matching a *specific* individual to a particular group. Finding the right community group that will suit an individual can be easy, but it can also be quite tricky. There are a number of matters that need to be well thought through before introducing an individual to a group. This chapter will:

- explain how to locate a suitable group for a specific individual with long-term disability
- identify issues to be considered before introducing the person to the group
- list important factors that contribute to a good match
- describe the process of supporting a person to attend the first group meeting.

Finding the right group for an individual

Sometimes a person has a very specific interest which seemingly cannot easily be met by general interest groups such as seniors' groups. The TTR coordinator then needs to carry out a more targeted search in response to that interest. For example, Stephen's interest in history initially led to a dead end because all the local historical settings and museums we found were inundated with volunteers, so there were very long waiting lists. Eventually, a community garden located on an historic site was found and Stephen decided he liked it. This garden offered many opportunities in addition to gardening, as the site was being gradually restored by the council. Previously inaccessible areas were opening up, old coal carts were going to be restored, an environmental centre was being built next door, and there were plans for some chickens to form part of the community garden. So, Stephen's interest in local history was still accommodated at a great site that was not an immediately obvious choice when looking for a group involving history.

 Stephen (0:42–1:45)
   Retirement lifestyle planning meeting

The TTR coordinator meets with Stephen and his mother at home. She explains Stephen's interest in history.

 Stephen (1:46–2:18)
   Matching the group and the person

The TTR coordinator describes the match between the Coal Loader Garden and Stephen's interest in history.

Checking suitability – before an introduction

It is important to make sure that the group has the potential to work for the person with disability before you take them for an introduction.

One example from the TTR project was Charlie who wanted to volunteer at a soup kitchen – we contacted the local soup kitchen whose group leader was against having a male volunteer at her all-female kitchen. While we could have argued our case based on rights, frankly there was little chance of this working well for Charlie as the group ap-

5 Locating a group for an individual

peared to have already made their mind up about refusing to have any males join their ranks.

You need to ask yourself the following practical questions. If there are too many negatives then it is possible that the group will not be feasible:

- How is the person going to travel to the group?
- How will the person travel back home from the group?
- How much does it cost – can the person afford it?
- Does the day of the week fit with the person's workdays and other commitments?
- Are there any issues of accessibility that need to be considered?
- Does the group have any rules that are likely to cause a problem? Some groups are funded by a single local council, so group members need to live within that local government area to attend – just because a group is close, does not always mean that a person is eligible to attend!

Although these issues can create practical difficulties, we found that with creativity and cooperation many such problems could be overcome. The prime focus should be on giving the person with disability a well-supported chance to join a suitable community group, and wherever possible these practical problems should be solved.

Ken volunteers at the aviation museum

Ken has been fascinated by aeroplanes since he was a child and this was his main area of interest. We found an aviation museum located some 50 km away on the other side of the city that always welcomed new volunteers. However, the key question was – how was Ken going to get there? The TTR coordinator investigated options and the journey would take two hours and involve a bus from home to the train station, a train to a major city junction, a second bus journey taking him near the museum, and then a short walk from the bus stop to the museum. The reason that this opportunity was successful was that Ken already had good travel skills and was eager to learn a new route. Because of the complexity of this trip, if Ken had not possessed these skills then this group would not have been feasible for him.

Ken at the Aviation Museum

A good match

Assuming that it is feasible for the person to go to the group(s) you have found, the next issue is trying to achieve the best possible match between the person and the group. A good match is fundamental to future success. Judging the match involves several issues:

- **Interests.** Does the group offer activities that are of interest to the person and which the person is able to take part in, with support as needed? For example, some groups involve a lot of conversation and little practical activity. This group may not be a good match for a person who does not enjoy conversation or has very limited verbal communication skills.
- **Gender.** Many groups cater for both men and women but some groups are gender specific.
- **Age/frailty.** All the groups we found catered for older people, but some involved more vigorous physical activity (e.g., walking, sport) and so were better suited to more robust individuals. Other groups were set up for frail aged people and offered more sedentary activity

plus other supports (e.g., door-to-door transport, nutritious cooked lunch).
- **Group culture.** There are a number of issues to think about regarding the "culture" of the group. Many of these issues can only be understood by spending time with the group, observing activities and talking to members. Pay attention to how people dress, what they do together or individually, how they interact, what they talk about, and their style of speaking. For example do people tease and joke, is swearing acceptable?

In judging the group's culture you need to ask yourself the following "gut feeling" questions:

- Is the person's personality likely to clash the group? Some people can be loud, boisterous or swear, so a quiet ladies' knitting group might not be the best match.
- Will the person's topics of conversation or behaviours be perceived as too unusual for the group? Talking about sports such as football fits in well in some groups but not in others. Some people with long-term disability have repetitive behaviours or language use which some group members may find difficult.
- Is the size of the group likely to cause any difficulty? Some people are very shy and so a large group is likely to be challenging for them – see Bronwyn's story below.
- Does the group appear to have rules too rigid to enable any needed flexibility for a person with disability? Some groups are very structured and rule-driven – if routines need to be adapted for a person with long-term disability to participate then it is likely that this will cause stress within the group.
- Are there social routines within the group, often with unwritten rules, that need to be considered? For example, do people take turns at bringing in snacks for morning tea? If so, is it feasible to support the person with long-term disability to do this when his/her turn comes around?
- Are there group members who have experience of being around people with disability (e.g., a family member)?

Introduction to the group

> *Bronwyn's first visit does not go well*
>
> Bronwyn really enjoyed craft, knitting and crochet and felt that a group with these activities would be of interest to her. The local senior citizens' centre held a small craft group each Tuesday morning for one hour before a much larger group met for games and entertainment. The group seemed a perfect fit, but we didn't make enough allowance for Bronwyn's shy personality. On the planned day to introduce Bronwyn the usual staff member was sick and so a casual staff member replaced this person and met the TTR coordinator at the seniors' centre. Suddenly, Bronwyn was faced with a situation where she was with a relatively unknown staff member, in a foreign environment, and there were far too many people for her liking. Suffice to say, Bronwyn never went back to this group. We didn't prepare an introduction sufficiently that matched Bronwyn's personality and needs.

As Bronwyn's story shows, an introduction can go wrong if not planned carefully and done well. The person with disability needs as much information as possible about the introduction, without being overwhelmed with too much detail. The types of things that he/she needs to know include:

- What day and what time the introduction is. You may need to help the person put this on a calendar.
- Where is the group situated? You may need to drive by one day to show the person the building and location.
- How will the person with disability travel to the group? You may need to let staff and family know what time you will meet the person.
- Who will the person meet at the group? You may need to tell the person the group leader's name and a little bit about them.
- What are they likely to do at the group? You may need to prepare the person by providing a summary. For example: arrive, sign in, morning tea, meet some people, look at the types of activities, and then go home.

5 Locating a group for an individual

- What style of dress is appropriate? Does the person need to bring anything or any money?

At the first group meeting

Unless the person has lots of self-confidence, then it is always a good idea to be side by side with the person during the introduction.

 Tip

Allow at least one hour for an introduction to the group.

The things that you will need to do to support the person with long-term disability at an introduction will vary, but there are some basics that you will almost always need to do. These are:

1. *Signing in and paying any money* – all groups have a register of attendees and this usually means signing a book. If the group also has weekly fees, the money is usually collected at sign in. So, it is wise to have the correct amount of money prepared to avoid any difficulties with large notes and change.
2. *Introduction to key group members* – this will need to be courteous and as formal as the group requires. The person with long-term disability is likely to need close support for this procedure, as it can be daunting at first.
3. *Morning or afternoon* tea – almost every group gets together for a tea break. This is a good time to visit the group as it is often one of the most social times and one where the person with disability can meet many of the group members while sharing a cup of coffee and a biscuit. Again, you may need to offer the person with disability significant support during this time, particularly if the person has limited social and/or communication skills.

> **Tip**
>
> Don't talk about the person with disability as if they are not present. Do redirect any questions from group members about the person to the person, while still giving needed support (e.g., remind the person to mention important details).

4. *Key message* – the core message that you are supporting the person to get across is that they are no different from anyone else and they are simply looking around to see if they are keen to join the group.
5. *Opportunity to look around and try an activity* – once the tea break is over, try to identify if a particular group member shows interest in the person with disability. This may be the person who was sitting next to them during the tea break. Usually someone stands out as being more engaged with the new person with disability at this initial meeting. Suggest that this group member show the person around the group, to give a tour of possible activities, and to perhaps even try an activity together.
6. *Make yourself scarce if you can* – while the person is being shown around, this is the perfect time to step back and allow the group to do what it would do for any prospective new member. This also gives you a chance to strategically chat to key group members. Often there will be group members with specific questions or concerns and they usually do not hesitate to ask them.
7. *Say your goodbyes* – once the person has been shown around, and particularly if you get a sense that they have had enough, then it is a good time leave. Make it clear what the next step is, for example – "Graeme and I will go away and talk about the group and get back to you if Graeme is keen to come again".

Trying out different groups

Some people recommend visiting several different groups – this is sometimes known as activity sampling – before choosing one to try. This approach gives the person a real choice. We can see the benefits of

5 Locating a group for an individual

this idea, but in our TTR study in most cases we only introduced the person to a second group, if he/she had decided not to go ahead with joining the first group visited. Most of our participants chose to join the first group they were introduced to and have continued to go to that group for several years now.

6
A new routine

Attending a community group one day per week instead of working necessarily involves a change in routine. On the community group day, the person with long-term disability:

- goes to a different place using different travel arrangements
- leaves home at a different time
- takes part in different activities
- may need different clothing, equipment or money
- has different people providing any needed support.

These changes may have spill-over effects into other parts of the person's life because the new routine may affect other people at home or at work. The TTR program seeks to build on the strengths of predictable routines by having the person go to the group at the same time and in the same place each week. Even so, the process of creating a new routine needs time, effort and cooperation from all concerned. Transition will only be successful with support at home and at work.

Mapping a new routine is all about changing current routines to accommodate the new lifestyle on the day(s) when person with long-term disability goes to the community group. For many people with disability, this is perhaps the first time they have been involved in their community as an individual with no support from family or disability staff.

Depending on where people live, how they travel to the community group of their choice and what they do there, major areas of their life will be affected, requiring changes for:

- the individual
- home life – family and/or accommodation service
- work life – employment service
- community group
- travel.

This chapter describes the many components of mapping a new routine that affect various areas of the person's life. Detailed examination of travel training is set out in Appendix A.

Changes for the individual

Mapping a new routine for a person with long-term disability requires a hands-on approach. The degree of help and the amount of support time needed is based on the person's skills, confidence and social circumstances. Each person's transition is tailored to his/her individual needs. To maintain each person's independence, support is given only when needed.

Examples of support provided to the individual include:

- **Skills** (e.g., time telling, recognising signs and landmarks, new activities)
- **Buying/taking appropriate clothes** (e.g., wet weather gear, hat)
- **Planning new travel routes** including planning the simplest, safest route
- **Re-assessing finances** (e.g., making a decision about affordability – working out the impact of reduced wages, group participation and travel costs)
- **Money handling** including coin/note recognition, fares, and weekly group fees
- **Social etiquette** (e.g., appropriate community behaviour, politeness)
- **Communication tools** (e.g. identity card with phone numbers and vital health information; chat book with personal photos)
- **Travel training** (see below and Appendix A).

6 A new routine

In some cases it can take time to gain trust from the person with long-term disability that the changes made will be beneficial and in line with what he/she wishes. It can also take time for the person to feel safe about making changes to their routine. Reassurance is key for any change.

Interested but apprehensive

Judy is 64, lives in a group home, enjoys domestic activities and art, and has limited speech. Due to recent health concerns, family and group home staff talked with Judy about dropping a day of work and joining a community group. Although Judy was apprehensive she expressed an interest in trying other activities through the week.

The TTR coordinator, Nicolette, provided many weeks of support and reassurance by going to Judy's house once a week and spending time with her. This helped Nicolette to establish a level of trust and allowed her to get to know Judy's likes and dislikes, her routine, the things she's good at and activities she enjoys, as well as learning different ways of communicating with her.

Nicolette found a potential group for Judy and then created a photo booklet to show Judy the community group building, the types of activities she would do when she's there and some of the members' faces. Each week Nicolette spent some time talking about the community group by using the booklet until Judy indicated she would like to visit the group.

After the initial visit, Judy told staff she would like to keep going to the group. Nicolette arranged an official start date and they attended for several months together until Judy was comfortable. Because Nicolette had taken the time to get to know Judy, she was able to educate the community group as to how best communicate with Judy in order to create solid relationships within the centre.

Nicolette's picture booklet formed the basis of Judy's photo booklet, which Judy takes to the group every week and which everyone uses with Judy to support communication.

Judy and her new friends look at her photo booklet

> 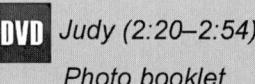 *Judy (2:20–2:54)*
> *Photo booklet*
>
> In this scene Judy initiates conversation by showing pictures of her family, friends and interests to members of the group. Judy uses this booklet to introduce herself to members. The booklet also offers a way for them to get to know her and talk with her.

Changes to home life (the family)

When a person with long-term disability is living with family, changing routine is usually straightforward and is negotiated directly with the person and family members involved. If the person with disability is living with parents they are likely to be retired and to have the time to be flexible when providing support. Family members are usually highly motivated to support the person with disability to develop a retirement lifestyle. As well, they want to be confident that they have something in place for the future. When family members support the transition, things often run smoothly and don't require as much negotiation as when a person is living in a group home or other accommodation provided by a disability service.

If the person with disability is living with a sibling or a person who is working, it may be harder for the family member to be flexible enough to provide all the needed support, so some other arrangements may be necessary (e.g., support to travel to the group).

Family may need to assist with:

- transport (e.g., driving the person to the group; prompting the person to leave home at the correct time)
- money (e.g., providing the correct money each week to person or re-organising their budget)
- reminding the person of upcoming events at the community group (e.g., taking needed clothing or equipment; changes in routine for one-off events)
- setting up communication between home and the community group about events, special needs and who to advise if the person with disability will be absent or if for some reason the group session is cancelled
- providing encouragement and showing interest (e.g., asking the person with disability about what happened at the group; sometimes visiting the group).

Changes to home life (the accommodation service)

This aspect can be quite lengthy. Discussions and communication often involve a range of accommodation staff (case workers and various managers), as well as family. There can be initial enthusiasm by staff for the TTR program but actually implementing some changes can involve extended consultation. Adjusting longstanding fixed routines at the accommodation service can be difficult because changes may also affect other residents and staff. Despite everyone wanting the best for the person in the TTR program, negotiations can be complex, and it is not always easy to resolve issues (see Table 6.1).

Table 6.1 Practical issues to be worked through when adjusting routines involving the accommodation service

Issue	Problem	Possible solutions
Staff shifts	Staff morning shifts are set up assuming that all residents leave early (before 8 am) for work, but the person does not leave until 9.45 am to go to the community group.	The person learns to stay home alone. Extra staffing provided on that day. Another arrangement is set up to ensure the person is safe.
Transport	Other residents need transport and must be dropped off at specific times. The person needs to be dropped at the community group later and at a different location from workdays.	The house's drop-off schedule is reorganised so the person is dropped off last at the community group. Other travel arrangements are made and supported (e.g., travel training, taxi).
New staff responsibilities	The person needs support to be ready to go to the group and with being aware of special group events.	Staff and management set up systems to deal with communication to and from the community group. Helping the person to be ready on time with all needed items.
Internal communication	Details about going to the group can change from week to week.	Written internal staff communication systems are used to record these details and communicate them as needed.

6 A new routine

It takes a lot of work negotiating these important details and often the solutions can't be implemented straight away.

> *Professor Roger Stancliffe (3:35–4:54)*
> *Service providers working and planning together*
>
> Roger Stancliffe points out that many people with disability use more than one disability service (e.g., employment service and group home), often with each service operated by a different agency. Transition to retirement represents a major change in the person's life that affects all service providers, so the planning process takes time and can be complex.

Overcoming constraints

When you have a dedicated retirement team, the team can help alter some of the old routines that are no longer consistent with the person's new needs. The TTR team can assist in mapping a new routine concerning:

- transport
- liaison/communication between the key people in the person with long-term disability's life
- keeping a clear focus on the person's wishes and needs and providing support to overcome hesitations about change.

Sam goes dancing

Sam wanted to go to a dancing group but relied solely on community-living staff for transport as he was unable to learn to travel independently. The group's finish time was outside normal staff working hours, so Sam was not able to go.

The TTR coordinator took Sam to and from the group for a month until staff negotiated with management to extend staff hours

---

> on the day Sam went dancing. He is now travels to and from the group with staff and is enjoying learning how to dance.

The TTR coordinator should not to be relied upon for long-term assistance. However the coordinator can often be a buffer, because the first few weeks of support are provided as one-to-one at the community group. Even so, it is important to have long-term arrangements in place as early as possible to help the person with disability to get used to the routine and gain independence.

 Tip

The person doesn't need to attend a community group for a full day. A more relaxed pace of life is just as important as community engagement. In fact participants in our research project averaged 3.6 hours per day at their group, not counting travel time.

 Stephen (4:57–5:18)

Sleeping in

Stephen's mother describes how he enjoys not having to get up so early on the day he goes to the community garden.

Changes for work life (the employment service)

Arranging to drop or swap the person's required day at work is relatively easy in cases where the retirement program is provided by the same service provider as the employment service. The TTR team work directly with management and clerical staff to adjust working hours. Often this doesn't take place formally until the person is certain that he/she wants to remain at the chosen community group. We found this usually happens within a month of trial visits. During this time it is up to the employment service as to whether to pay the person for their normal hours of work or to ask the person to take paid leave for each day off, or to reduce the pay straight away and finalise the paperwork at a later date. These issues need to be discussed clearly so the person knows the effect on his/her wages and leave entitlements.

Areas of concern for the person or the disability employment service can involve:

- **Funding** – regulations around minimum number of work hours for retention of government funding per person/block funding – making sure that these rules are understood and followed. In these cases workdays may need to be changed to ensure the minimum hours of work are met.
- **Employment benefits** – impact on wages of changing from full-time to part-time work, and on accumulation of annual leave and sick leave.
- **Productivity** – the effect on the employment service's output when the person isn't there.
- **Vacancies** – creating opportunities for younger employees to take the working place of an older employee on his/her day off.

Some assistance from the employment service may need to be set up if the person attends their community group directly from work.

Alexander goes bowling

Alexander wanted to go bowling on a Thursday afternoon, but he still wanted to maximise his working hours for financial reasons, so he continued to work on Thursday mornings.

To set up Alexander's new routine, the TTR team arranged for Alexander to join the earlier lunch break group at work on Thursdays so he wouldn't miss his bus. The TTR team also organised with his work supervisors to remind Alexander when it was time to leave work so he could walk down the road to catch his bus on time.

Stephen signs in at his group

Changes for the community group

Mapping a new routine also involves assistance with change at the community group. Establishing a new routine is easier with support from one or more 'mentors' at the community group (Chapter 7). Mentors volunteer to take on a specific role in supporting the person with disability while at the group. Mentors have proven to be vital in the sustainability of the person attending the group.

Establishing a new routine at a community group can be as simple as asking a mentor to support the person to sign in, or arranging for the person to have someone to sit with at morning tea or lunch. Some changes may involve other group members and so require some negotiation. For example, Judy's new role of setting the tables for lunch (see Judy's story on the DVD) had to be discussed with those who had set the tables in the past. They needed to agree to stand back and leave the task to Judy and her mentor. In the early weeks, occasionally someone would forget and start laying the tablecloths, only to receive a friendly reminder from the mentor – "There's no need to set the table, Judy does that now". As well as providing satisfaction for the person with disability, such positive involvement gives that person a valued role within the group, and helps build acceptance of the person with disability as a fully contributing group member.

Another fundamental part of the routine at the community group involves respecting local custom and practice. Signing in on arrival is a common expectation at many groups. On the other hand, after morning tea practices differ about what to do with the dirty crockery and who washes up (e.g., at some groups people wash their own cups, at other groups people take turns to wash up all cups). Ensuring that the person with disability knows and follows the community group's customs helps establish a routine that promotes ready acceptance by group members. This issue is discussed in more detail in Chapter 7.

In groups where a lot of time is spent in conversation, some people with disability may find it difficult to join in beyond a few familiar conversation topics. There are several ways to structure the person's routine to respond to this issue:

- ask a mentor to help the person use concrete conversation supports (the person's photo album/chat book from home; looking at a magazine together and talking about stories/photos of interest)
- schedule a practical activity for the person with disability with some other group members during times when conversation is the main group activity for most members
- support the person to bring in a preferred activity from home that can be done independently or with others during conversation time (e.g., knitting, card game, craft activity). It is important that this should be an activity that is appropriate within the culture of the group.

One final issue is ensuring that the person with disability has enough to do, and does not become bored or isolated. The person may not have the necessary skills (e.g., literacy) to take part in all of the activities available at the group, so the TTR coordinator needs to be vigilant in identifying activities that the person is able to do or learn. Indeed, it may be necessary to modify some activities or even create new ones, or provide specific support so that the activity is within the person's capacities. For example, Joanne could knit reasonably well, but was not able to cast on, so a mentor did this for her. She also needed someone to keep an eye on making sure that each row had the same number of stitches. Chng et al. (2013) presented an example where supporting mentors in introducing new craft activities resulted in a substantial increase in the person's participation in activities, thus ensuring that she had enough to do.

In some cases the person with disability and the mentors choose to write down the person's routine at the group in an informal list of activities available (e.g., see a short scene in Stephen's story on the DVD [3:40–3:57] where Stephen is assisted to check the list of gardening tasks he is responsible for).

Helping the person and the mentors to correctly set up these routines at the group enables the person with disability to become a contributing and accepted member of the group with the same rights and responsibilities as everyone else. Setting up routines can also involve encouraging the person to join particular subgroups within their community group that align with their traits and interests.

 Cedric (4:54–5:32)

Establishing routines within the group

Every week, as soon as Cedric arrives he signs in, makes a cup of tea and then joins the 'Old men's table' – a recognised subgroup within the seniors' centre. This is an example of a person who has established a routine with the initial assistance of his mentor and now fits in with everyone else.

Communication between the community group and home

The TTR team needs to put into place methods of formalising communication between caregivers/family and the community group. One example was by encouraging the exchange of email addresses between the community group and the person with disability's niece. All membership correspondence is provided not only to the person with disability but also emailed to the niece who in turn informs and reminds her uncle. Other community groups simply send home a note with the person with the information to be communicated back to carers/family. An exchange of phone numbers is also helpful (e.g., so there is someone to call for help if the person's transport home does not arrive).

When mapping a new routine, the TTR team always encourage key stakeholders in the person's life to attend the community group and form their own relationships with mentors and other group members. This leads to a smoother initial transition and fewer misunderstandings arising from lack of communication. Together with the ongoing support of mentors and monitoring by the TTR coordinator, such direct relationships between these stakeholders and community group members contribute to the long-term success of the person attending their group.

Travel

Attending a community group necessarily involves travel. Very few people with disability have their own car, so most rely on other people or on public transport. Travel can be seen as a barrier that may prevent the person from attending a group, but our experience has been that this issue could always be dealt with provided some effort and creativity were used in coming up with a solution (Bigby et al., in press). The TTR coordinator is often involved in investigating travel options and helping to create a workable long-term solution.

Participants in our research project used a variety of transport methods to travel to and from their group activity, depending on the location of the group, the availability of a ride from staff, family or friends, the accessibility of suitable public transport and the person's ability to learn to travel independently, or the availability of transport provided by the community group itself (e.g., a community minibus) (Bigby et al., in press). Our research participants travelled by:

- walking
- public transport (bus and/or train)
- taxi
- car/van driven by disability staff
- car/van/minibus provided by the community group
- car driven by family member or friend.

In some circumstances a different form of transport was used for the return journey (e.g., because public transport was not running at the time needed). Once again, this was an issue to be dealt with, and a solution was found. A few participants sometimes were given a ride in a group member's car for part or the entire journey home after the group meeting, but this support was often intermittent, so a primary means of travel home was still needed.

Other appropriate forms of transport, which were not used by our research participants, include – bicycle, mobility scooter, community transport, and recruiting a volunteer driver.

Travel training

Travel training is a major component of mapping a new routine for a number of people with long-term disability. These new skills give the person greater access to and involvement in the community and increase independence.

Learning a new travel route is empowering. The confidence and freedom to travel independently helps the person with disability access other local activity options. For example, initially Laurie learned to travel by bus to a nearby suburban CBD to sing in the community choir, but some two years after the DVD was shot he uses the same travel skills to volunteer at a seniors' centre on Fridays and play lawn bowls on Saturdays. In each case the same bus journey is involved, so Laurie's travel skills have opened up new opportunities for him. The time invested in teaching Laurie to travel has paid off, with no additional travel training being needed when supporting him to volunteer at the seniors' centre.

> *Laurie (3:25–4:05)*
>
> <u>Benefits of travel training</u>
>
> In this scene Melwyn explains the benefits of Laurie independently travelling to take part in the community choir. As Laurie says: "I don't need the staff to say 'Laurie would you like a hand catching the bus?' No thank you! I'm capable of catching it on my own."

Some people may be using public transport for the first time. For others it may be a case of learning to use a different type of transport (e.g., trains as well as buses). For some, travel training may involve mastering a new travel route on an already familiar type of public transport. The amount of assistance needed depends on the individual's existing experience, skills and level of confidence, as well as the complexity of the trip. Consequently, one-to-one training support will be needed for as long as it takes for the person to master the new journey.

Travel training is complex. Appendix A provides information about how to provide travel training and gives examples drawn from parts of Graeme's trip to the community plant nursery.

Final thoughts on routines

There are many things to think about when helping a person with a long-term disability to make changes in his/her daily routine. A smooth and successful transition requires careful consideration of the person's wishes, needs, abilities and circumstances, and support should be tailored to reflect this. It's often best to minimise the disruptions by changing only what is necessary in the person's current routine.

Paramount to the success of the person's transition is building strong relationships with people in all aspects of his/her life, including the new social contacts at the community group.

 Tip

Think creatively, offer solutions, be accommodating and where possible provide support not only to the person but also to their caregivers/family members, staff in their workplace and the community group.

Other examples of mapping a new routine
- Assisting the person to order a name badge or uniform so he/she looks like and feels like the other members

- Setting up supports to ensure the person has the correct equipment each week (e.g., bowling shoes, sun protection)
- Establishing an effective system to enable the person to take the correct money (e.g., envelopes with exact change if need be)
- Setting up reminder prompts through family/staff/community group members (e.g., for one-off events, special occasions, absences)
- Teaching basic mobile phone skills for those learning to travel independently
- Talking about boundaries with socialising (e.g., personal space, appropriate conversation topics)
- Introducing the person and providing other members with some basic background/interests of person and ensuring the person has support to engage in conversations with group members.

Modifying routines over time

Even when a new routine is established successfully, it may well change over time. Maintaining a workable routine needs regular communication with the person with disability, accommodation staff/family and community group members in order to identify any need for change and to help all those affected work through any changes (see Chapter 8).

7
Recruiting and training mentors

Why choose mentors when other approaches are also available to support the person with long-term disability to attend a community group? One option is for an external disability expert to directly support the person at the group, gradually fading out the support over time – akin to the job coach model in mainstream employment support. However, our approach was to recruit and train mentors from among group members – similar to the co-worker support model in mainstream employment where co-workers of the person with disability volunteer to provide on-the-job support and these co-workers are in turn supported and trained by a disability job coach (Farris & Stancliffe, 2001; Wilson et al., 2010).

 Professor Roger Stancliffe (1:54–2:31)
   Recruiting and training mentors

Roger Stancliffe explains what mentors do. There is a short scene showing one part of mentor training.

> **DVD** *Dr Nathan Wilson (1:41–2:48)*
>
> <u>The reason we use mentors</u>
>
> Nathan Wilson explains that mentors are long-term group members, and can provide ongoing support to the person with long-term disability. Being group members themselves, mentors can also greatly enhance the person's social inclusion within the group in a way that an outside disability professional would find difficult.

The "natural" support provided by mentors has many advantages:

- mentors are always present and so can provide support whenever it is needed
- by their involvement mentors promote social inclusion
- mentors are insiders who are familiar with the culture of the group and so can "show the new person the ropes" in a way that enables that person to become an accepted member of the group
- mentors are usually part of the local community so there can be additional incidental social contact outside the group (e.g., bumping into a mentor at the local shopping centre)
- mentors learn about disability by getting to know an individual and in doing so, help create more positive community attitudes
- mentors are volunteers and so make it possible for the person with long-term disability to receive long-term one-on-one support at little cost.

> <u>Mentors getting to know the person with disability</u>
>
> "he's very kind and he's got a lovely sense of humour and he will really pitch in . . . he's delightful to have around really"
>
> Comment by a mentor

7 Recruiting and training mentors

Recruiting mentors

Typically we began to recruit mentors after the person with long-term disability had been to the group with the coordinator for several weeks. This approach was meant to:

- give the person time to get to know the group and its members and to make sure that he/she was comfortable with the group
- give group members a chance to engage with the person
- give the TTR coordinator time to observe opportunities for participation, which group members chose to interact with the person and the nature of those interactions.

Before beginning to recruit mentors it is often appropriate to talk to the group leaders about mentoring, how best to approach potential mentors, and to ask group leaders for suggestions about whom to ask to be a mentor.

> *Mentoring is an opportunity*
>
> "the opportunity to be able to work with somebody like that ... it doesn't come your way frequently"
>
> Comment by a mentor

The most appropriate mentors are usually those who naturally gravitate to assisting the person with disability and who display a positive, accepting attitude. They should be members who are not planning to leave the group (e.g., moving interstate) and who regularly attend the group on the day the person with disability comes. Likewise, it is important that the person with disability relates comfortably to the mentors and is willing to share activities and social interactions with them. Other desirable characteristics may include:

- shared interests (e.g., knitting, singing, making things)
- matching gender and/or cultural and language background can be helpful in some cases.

Approaching possible mentors can require breaking down any apprehensions they may have about how to support a person with long-term disability. Reassure mentors by pointing out that their role is to provide straightforward everyday help, not to be "social workers", and that training and ongoing support will be provided by the TTR co-ordinator.

> *Dr Nathan Wilson (0:44–1:39)*
> *Recruiting mentors and creating realistic expectations*
>
> Nathan Wilson explains why the TTR program makes use of mainstream community groups. He also discusses ensuring that members of the group who are potential mentors have accurate expectations about their role as a mentor, which involves providing uncomplicated support for the person with disability to participate in the group's activities.

We found that often mentors were happy to volunteer but did not want to be the only one. As one person explained, "If I cannot be here one week, I don't want to feel guilty that she will miss out." If there are other mentors involved they can share the role and there will always be someone around to give support, even if one of the mentors is absent.

We had no difficulty in finding volunteers to be mentors (Wilson et al., 2013). Many people seemed willing to help but were unsure what to do. However, they felt more confident knowing that they would receive expert training and support. The ease of recruitment may also have been because the scope of the mentor's role was limited to support for familiar activities, in a well-known setting, for a few hours once a week.

Training mentors

We provided two complementary forms of training for mentors (Bigby et al., in press):

- **Disability Interaction Training** (one session involving all mentors, and often all group members)

- **Hands-on training** (multiple short coaching sessions with individual mentors when activities occurred naturally).

Disability Interaction Training

The aim of this session was to demystify long-term disability and to help mentors to begin to plan appropriate activities and effective support for the person with long-term disability in their group. The training session ran for an average of one hour, involved all the mentors from that group participating together, and was delivered where the group met at a convenient time for mentors (usually before, during or after the group's regular activities). In many instances the person with disability also took part in this session, but this was not always the case. Their involvement depended on their preference about taking part and on judgements about the appropriateness of such involvement (e.g., how comfortable they would be being the focus of attention and discussion).

We developed a Disability Interaction Training package involving short video clips and printed notes summarising key points on the issues set out in Table 7.1. When training mentors, the TTR coordinator needs to bring along enough printed copies of the notes for each mentor, and have the laptop (with projector if necessary for larger groups) and speakers set up ready before training starts.

Discussion about these topics was tailored to focus on the personal qualities and specific support needs of the person with disability joining the group. A number of DVD clips were used as discussion points to demystify long-term disability, introduce person-centred principles and focus on the different ways to support a person with long-term disability. The conversation often moved on to wider discussion about the group, the range of available activities, the possibilities for the person to take part in those activities, and how mentors could best support that participation.

Table 7.1. Topics covered in the Disability Interaction Training package

Topic	Content
Disability in Australia	Different types of disabilities and the support people need to remain active and take part in their community.
What language do we use?	How to use People First Language.
What do people with disability expect?	People with a long-term disability expect to be treated no differently from anyone else. They want to have the same opportunities as others.
Support from others	Some people with long-term disability need practical assistance from others to fully take part in their community.
Interacting with people who have disability	Interact with a person with long-term disability in a way that reflects their age. Speak directly to the person and not through their carer, friend or family member.
Some specific disabilities	Brief information on intellectual disability, physical disability and mental illness.
Older people with disability.	People with a long-term disability want to enjoy their retirement but may need some help to do the things they want in retirement.

Listed below is a selection of currently available videoclips from among those we used during Disability Interaction Training (all links were correct at the time of writing).

- **Video clip "Shopmobility"** (duration 3:33) – from the You Can Volunteer DVD series by Mencap (UK). Shows Paul Brannick, a volunteer with Shopmobility Manchester assisting people with mobility problems to move around the shops. Paul is a man with intellectual disability. Video clip is available at www.youtube.com/watch?v=kMUYw04cAtc

7 Recruiting and training mentors

- **Video clip "Nicole volunteering at the community kitchen"** (5:15–5:42) – from the DVD *Inclusion Melbourne: people creating better lives* (duration of entire DVD 14:37). This video contains several other very useful stories (e.g., Jeremy joining Melbourne AFL football club's cheer squad). The video is available at www.inclusionmelbourne.org.au/about-us/our-video/.

Of course, we recommend that readers also use selected scenes from the *Transition to retirement* DVD that accompanies this manual as a resource for mentor training.

 Judy (2:54–3:43)
Mentors' Disability Interaction Training

This scene shows Roger leading a Disability Interaction Training session with a group of mentors. The laptop and speakers on the table were for showing the brief DVD clips. You will also notice the printed notes that each mentor was given. Note that the discussion is individualised around the person with disability (in this case Judy) and her specific interests and support needs. In Judy's case part of the discussion centres on practical activities to share as an alternative to conversation, because Judy's speech is limited.

One key idea to communicate during all mentor training is that the person with disability should be given many opportunities for social interaction and participation in activities, with support as needed. Naturally, the person should be able to choose whether, when and how to take part (Stancliffe, Wilson et al., 2013). It is essential that mentors understand that, without support and encouragement, the person with long-term disability may find it difficult to take the initiative to join in because of a lack of confidence, or limited social or practical skills. Without support, the person may become bored and socially isolated.

> ### Mentors supporting inclusion
>
> "[you've got to] prepare her beforehand ... just because she doesn't speak ... telling her what's going on ... even if it's two or three weeks in a row"
>
> *Comment by a mentor*

Ideally, the Disability Interaction Training session should finish with several concrete ideas about new activities and/or how to implement effective support for existing activities, with a plan to begin to use these ideas the next time the person with disability comes to the group. Where appropriate, an informal written timetable of activities may be helpful. The TTR coordinator can type up the agreed schedule and bring back printed copies the following week. At the end of the training session, the TTR coordinator can arrange with each mentor to take part in an individual hands-on training session the next week.

Sometimes different mentors provide support for different activities. It is important to be clear about who is responsible for what. Be aware that the mentor's role is voluntary so all support has to be negotiated or suggested. Ideally, the choice of who will provide the support and the way that support will be given will be proposed by the mentors, with the TTR coordinator offering suggestions and feedback.

Hands-on training

Sometimes support can be as simple as having someone to sit with at morning tea, or a mentor showing the person with disability what to do in everyday situations at the group (e.g., where members put their bags, where the toilets are, where to make a cup of coffee). Most mentors need little training for this type of support, because it is the kind of introduction offered to new members regardless of ability.

7 Recruiting and training mentors

> **DVD** *Cedric (5:10–5:32)*
> <u>*Support with everyday group activities*</u>
>
> Cedric's mentor describes how she reminds him to sign in, put his money in the box and mentions that she showed him how to make a cup of tea, which he now does for himself.

People with long-term disability often have complex support needs, so the type and amount of support is not intuitively obvious to mentors. In these situations hands-on training is especially helpful. In a number of the examples that follow, we have focused on people with significant disability who have more extensive support needs, for example people with intellectual disability and limited verbal communication skills. This means that some of the suggestions later in this chapter may be too detailed for supporting individuals with milder disability, who may need little more than verbal explanations and reminders along with an occasional demonstration of what to do. The beauty of one-to-one hands-on training is that it can be customised to the individual support needs of the particular person with disability.

Active support

Many of the support techniques and training methods were drawn from an evidence-based approach known as Active Support (Wilson et al., 2010). Readers who would like more details about Active Support can consult a review article (Stancliffe et al., 2008) and a multimedia training manual (Mansell et al., 2005).

Hands-on training outcomes

For mentors, there are three main intended outcomes of hands-on training:

- Mentors give the person with disability more opportunities for participation in activities and/or social interaction.
- Mentors offer more support to the person (but only needed support).

- Mentors provide effective support that is likely to result in the person starting or continuing to participate.

The end result of mentor involvement should be increased participation by the person with disability.

Hands-on training procedures

Hands-on training typically involves one mentor at a time and takes place during the ordinary run of activities at the group in the weeks following the Disability Interaction Training. One important role for the TTR coordinator at the group is to notice opportunities for participation and/or support, and to quietly draw mentors' attention to these occasions, so that they can be used for hands-on training. That is, the training is often opportunistic, taking advantage of situations that arise naturally during the ebb and flow of activities. This approach has the benefit of seeming natural and of involving all of the typical conditions surrounding the activity at the group. Thus, hands-on mentor training is both practical and directly relevant to the way in which support for the person with disability will actually be provided in future. As a result, hands-on training is arguably the most important part of mentor training because it directly affects the way mentors provide support to the person at the group.

In addition to opportunistic hands-on training, new activities can be planned and implemented at an appropriate time and used for hands-on training. If there is an informal activity timetable for the person, the TTR coordinator can offer hands-on training by directing the mentor's attention to the timetable and asking the mentor to support the person with the next scheduled activity.

As the name suggests, hands-on training involves the mentor in directly supporting the person with long-term disability to take part in an activity while the TTR coordinator observes and provides coaching and feedback. Before the activity starts, the mentor and TTR coordinator may discuss the activity, how it is set up (e.g., what materials are needed) and how best to provide support. The following example illustrates this cycle of pre-activity discussion, coaching and planning; implementation of the activity with mentor support; and feedback to the mentor.

7 Recruiting and training mentors

> ### Leone reads a magazine
>
> Reading magazines was a common activity at Leone's seniors' group. The group kept a large supply on a bookshelf in a nearby room. The TTR coordinator pointed out to a mentor that Leone was sitting at her table with nothing to do. The coordinator suggested to the mentor that she:
>
> - ask Leone if she would like to read a magazine
> - show Leone where the magazines are kept
> - ask her to choose one
> - return with her to her table and spend a few minutes chatting about one or two of the magazine stories.
>
> The coordinator explained that providing support in this way (i.e., not getting the magazine for Leone) was an example of giving *just enough* support. In fact, Leone was learning how to bring back a magazine for herself. Added benefits included her choosing the magazine herself, plus having an enjoyable brief chat. Afterwards the coordinator and mentor discussed how the activity went and if the support was appropriate. As well, they talked about the possibility that in future weeks the support could be reduced further to a simply worded suggestion such as "Would you like to read a magazine Leone?"

Note that, in this example, the TTR coordinator also sensitises the mentor to look for relevant cues (i.e., noticing that Leone has nothing to do) in order to know *when* to intervene and when to suggest a new activity.

Recognising cues

The TTR coordinator should teach mentors to recognise other cues that are relevant to the person they are supporting. These may include – Signs of when support is needed:

- when the person is doing nothing and appears bored or withdrawn

- when the person is having difficulty with an activity or seems not to know what to do. Simplifying the activity may also help.
- when the person is socially isolated (e.g., sitting or standing alone).

Signs of when the person expects a familiar activity to begin but does not know when or how to start the activity and so needs either support to commence the activity or an explanation of why it is not possible at the moment:

- the person may go to the spot where the activity takes place and wait, or start gathering needed materials
- the person may approach the mentor who assists with that activity
- the person may sit or stand and look in the direction of the activity and/or needed materials.

Signs of when the person has had enough of an activity and needs a break or support to change to a different activity:

- the person may do one or more of the following – take off glasses, look away from activity, push materials away, sit back in chair, get up and walk away, put head down or appear sleepy.

These behaviours are more common in individuals with limited social and verbal skills. Such support may not be required if the person with disability can ask for a break, or enquire "Is it time for morning tea yet? I'm thirsty."

Mentors learning from one another

One mentor can serve as a role model for other mentors. In the next example, the TTR coordinator takes advantage of the good quality support given by one mentor to help other mentors understand some important features of first-class support.

Leone plays bingo – unobtrusive mentor support

Each week at Leone's seniors' group everybody played bingo. Leone was keen to take part and win prizes. Leone could recognise two-di-

> git numbers but sometimes missed a number and so failed to cross it off. This meant that she needed some inconspicuous mentor support if she was ever to win a prize. However, too much support could lead Leone or others to think that it was really the mentor who was playing for her.
>
> One mentor devised an effective but very unobtrusive means of support. She sat quietly next to Leone during bingo. If Leone missed a number the mentor would point to that number on Leone's bingo sheet to prompt Leone to cross it off. No verbal prompts or other support were needed. The TTR coordinator explained to the other mentors that this support approach was excellent because it provided *enough* support but not too much, it was clear and simple, it used a nonverbal cue and avoided complex language, and it was unobtrusive, so did not attract unnecessary attention to Leone.
>
> The TTR coordinator and mentors also came up with two simple adaptations to bingo to make the game easier for Leone. First, they asked the caller to slow down a little when calling the numbers to give Leone more time to find the number on her sheet. Second, they encouraged Leone to only use a single bingo sheet in each game although many other players in the group used multiple sheets simultaneously.
>
> Leone proudly reported that "I've won bingo once and won chocolate. I shared it with everybody else."

Coaching mentors to problem solve

As noted in Chapter 6, groups develop ways of doing things and have unwritten rules. To help the person with long-term disability fit into the group, mentors should try to be aware of these customs and support the person with disability to observe them. Judy's role of setting the tables at her group and the way this task was usually done provides a straightforward example of fitting in with local customs.

> ### Judy wears disposable gloves when setting the table
>
> With a mentor, Judy took on responsibility for setting the lunch tables for everybody at her group. When she began doing this task, nobody thought to tell her about wearing disposable gloves, so she was unaware that this was the group's usual practice. This continued for several weeks until the TTR coordinator overheard a remark from another group member and asked the mentor about this issue. The mentor responded that gloves were expected, so the coordinator suggested that the mentor ask Judy to wear gloves, and help her to put them on if necessary. The coordinator made it clear that unless the mentor explained simply to Judy that gloves are needed, she might never realise that this was the common practice. Judy's story on the DVD (3:43–4:01) demonstrates that Judy was perfectly happy to wear gloves and could put them on without assistance.

This situation also illustrates a common dilemma that mentors face. Unwritten rules are usually not talked about because most people pick up on them without being told. In turn, people are often uncomfortable in telling others explicitly to respect the 'in-house' rules and may assume that someone who fails to follow local customs does so intentionally. However, people with long-term disability, especially intellectual disability, often have restricted social experience, so their awareness of such norms may be limited. The TTR coordinator can help mentors understand that they will often need to provide explicit and direct support about not only what to do but also what *not* to do in order to help the person understand and fit in. Failure to do this keeps the person uninformed of these expectations. Continued violation of group expectations around different activities can cause other members to take offence. They may think that the person with disability is deliberately not following the usual practice. Without intervention, such situations can fester and may lead to the breakdown of the placement.

Within the group, the TTR coordinator should not intervene directly with the person with disability, but instead empower mentors to provide this support by:

- discussing any issues with mentors

- asking them to suggest how to deal with the issue
- if necessary, suggesting a way to approach the issue, including if needed recommending specific actions and a form of words (e.g., "Just before you start to set the tables take the box of gloves over to her and say 'When you set the table you should wear gloves, like me' and help her put the gloves on if she needsassistance.")

We encountered many other examples of people with disabilities unknowingly violating group norms – taking too many chocolate biscuits at morning tea; spending too long in the only available toilet. We supported mentors to help the person to act in more socially acceptable ways, usually by explaining what to do and why (e.g., "Only put two biscuits on your plate. Other people miss out if you eat too many;" "Hurry up please. Other people need to use the toilet.").

Tip

Always ask the mentor to provide support directly to the person. Do not do it yourself.

Effective support techniques

When coaching mentors about ways to provide effective support to a person with disability, bear in mind the following techniques:

- Before offering support, *wait* and see what the person can do unsupported.
- Make *one* request at a time (e.g., "Please get the wheelbarrow").
- Use tangible *cues* for people with difficulty understanding (e.g., use a box of disposable gloves as a cue for setting the table – see Judy's story).
- Don't talk too much. Instead use gesture (e.g., pointing) and demonstrate what to do, *one* step at a time, and then ask the person to imitate (see DVD clip from Graeme's story in the box below).
- Work at the person's own pace, don't rush.
- Use plenty or praise and encouragement.

Transition to retirement

Toby's mentor providing one-on-one direct support at the computer

- If there are difficult steps that the person is unable to do, either the mentor can complete the step (e.g., cast on the first row to begin knitting) as they work together on the activity, or the activity can be changed to avoid the difficult step. For example, Narelle had difficulty serving correctly in ping pong, so instead she hit the ball in her own way when it was her turn to serve.
- Have a predictable, consistent sequence of activities. Picture schedules, or for some people written schedules, may help a person know what to expect.
- Do activities in the same place, in the same way.
- Store materials in the same place (e.g., in Cedric's story on the DVD, when he makes his cup of tea all the needed items are always available in the same spot).

7 Recruiting and training mentors

Laurie singing at choir practice

> **DVD** *Graeme (3:37–3:50)*
> *Olympia teaches Graeme to pot plants*
>
> In this brief clip Graeme's mentor Olympia shows him how to pot seedlings. Note that she uses demonstration of one step at a time then waits for Graeme to imitate that step. One of the many advantages of demonstration is that it is easy to communicate just how and for how long to do the action.

Creative support solutions

Sometimes highly creative thinking is needed to support the person's participation. For example, whenever Laurie needed to learn a new song with his community choir, he was not helped by the choir members' typical practice of taking home the sheet music with the lyrics. Instead, a mentor came up with the idea of recording each song for Laurie, so that he could practise at home and learn each song by ear.

Rewards for mentors

Many mentors commented on the pleasure they gained from seeing the person with disability join in and grow in confidence at the group.

> *Graeme (3:15–3:38)*
> <u>Rewards for mentors</u>
>
> Olympia (mentor) comments on Graeme becoming more comfortable socially with other group members. She also mentions that seeing this growth is "the reward" for mentors.

8
Monitoring and ongoing support

Once a person with long-term disability has been going to a community group each week for some time and is participating in an array of activities with mentor support as needed, it is time for the TTR coordinator to begin to withdraw regular support. This gradual switch toward providing monitoring and ongoing support typically happens after five to ten weeks of attendance. This period varies a lot depending on the person's support needs and individual situation, as well as mentors' confidence. It is vital that all concerned clearly understand from the beginning that the TTR coordinator will be available long term to help when needed, BUT the coordinator's presence at the group will reduce over time to intermittent monitoring. The key to successful monitoring and ongoing support is timely, regular and effective communication, supplemented by on-site visits and support as needed.

For clarity, monitoring and ongoing support is presented in this manual as a distinct TTR program phase, but the transition from establishing a new routine (Chapter 7) is gradual. The TTR coordinator will go with the person to the group and stay for the entire time for the first few weeks. As parts of the new routine are bedded down, the coordinator should find reasons to slip away for a short period (e.g., 20 minutes, increasing over time). For example, if arriving at the group, signing in and paying fees is running smoothly, then the TRR coordinator may opt to come 20–30 minutes after the person has arrived. This will give all concerned the experience, during unchallenging periods, of getting along together without being able to seek immediate advice or reassurance from the TTR coordinator.

On the other hand, there can be parts of the routine that continue to be problematic (e.g., a promising activity that the person with disability finds difficult at first). If so, the coordinator may continue to attend the group briefly each week to assist solely with that activity until the difficulty is resolved. That issue apart, the rest of the person's time at the group is effectively operating in the monitoring phase without the TTR coordinator being present.

This chapter will present the benefits of monitoring and ongoing support and explain why they are needed. The chapter will also examine circumstances requiring a temporary increase in ongoing support, provide examples of different ways of structuring such support, and discuss dealing with problems that arise.

Benefits of ongoing support

Even the most successful matches between a person with long-term disability and a community group should never be taken for granted. Changes for the person or at the group will mean that there are new issues to deal with. Small issues can become big problems if they are not attended to promptly. Monitoring and ongoing support also offer positive benefits, including:

- Further opportunities for the person with long-term disability, the community group and the disability service offering the retirement program. For example, the senior's choir that Laurie joined sang at the disability service Christmas party and for various other community groups.
- The TTR coordinator is more aware of the changing activities taking place at the group each week and can therefore support mentors to help the person take advantage of new opportunities for participation as they arise.
- The TTR coordinator will hear about changes to the group's schedule. Some groups with a growing membership add another weekday for their activities. This gives the person the chance to go to the group twice a week. Alternatively, it could provide an opportunity

for another person with long-term disability to join the group on the new day.
- Greater support for the person with disability and his/her family.
- Mutually beneficial relationships can develop (cooperative approaches, leads to opportunities with other community groups, positive media releases, and stronger community links). For example, Judy's mentors nominated her for the local "Volunteer of the Year" awards – and she won.
- The person is more likely to remain in the community group long term.

 Shirley (4:09–4:56)

Mentors and support

Long-term participation in a community group can occur with the help of mentors. Catriona, one of Shirley's mentors, explains how she supports Shirley. TTR coordinator Nicolette talks about supporting mentors and other group members so that the person can be part of the group long term.

Reasons for ongoing monitoring and support

There will often be the need to support the person with long-term disability to deal with life changes. Change can affect the person directly, involve caregivers, or change can occur at the community group.

Changes affecting the person

Various factors can alter the person's life and so affect their routine at the community group. Examples include:

- *Health crisis and hospitalisation* – Chris had been volunteering at a soup kitchen for a year when he experienced an acute psychotic episode leading to hospitalisation and rehabilitation for several months. During that time he did not attend the soup kitchen. Without breaching Chris' privacy, the TTR team kept the community group abreast of Chris' absence, and maintained an open dialogue with Chris and his caregivers about his recovery and how best to support him to rejoin the group.

- *Minor health issues* – changes in diet (e.g., diabetes, allergies) may need to be communicated so mentors can help the person with diet at the group. Likewise, a minor work injury may need management while at the group (e.g., a person with a back strain may need to stand up and move after sitting for 30 minutes). Mentors may need guidance about how to support the person with this.
- *Change of residence* – Sophie had attended her local senior citizens' centre for two years but had to move out of her family home into supported accommodation in another suburb. The TTR coordinator supported Sophie with new routines and travel so she could continue to go to her community group.

Changes affecting caregivers

Caregivers play an important role in the person's life, so changes affecting caregivers in turn affect the person.

- *Caregiver crisis* – Tom had been going to his men's social group for over a year and a stable routine had been established where his father drove him to the group and had even started attending himself. Without warning, his father passed away. Tom needed support with bereavement and a new routine had to be set up. Prompt action by the TTR coordinator to arrange other transport resulted in Tom continuing to go to his group where he received compassionate support from other group members. In fact, several of the men from the group attended the funeral.
- *Staff turnover* – Julie had been going to her knitting group for two years and was well supported by her key worker who had worked at her group home for several years. Julie's key worker was rewarded for her expertise and promoted to a managerial position elsewhere. The TTR coordinator assisted Julie's new key worker to learn how to support Julie by attending the accommodation service team meeting to talk about the TTR program, and meeting one-on-one with Julie's

new key worker to discuss the kind of support Julie needed to attend her knitting group.

Changes affecting the community group

Just as individual lives change, so too a community group can face change and disruption.

- *Mentor leaving group* – Narelle had been going to the senior's activity centre for two years when a drop-in monitoring visit alerted the TTR coordinator to the fact that Narelle's key mentor had left the group. This had led to Narelle becoming disengaged. The TTR coordinator found a new mentor and trained that mentor how to provide just the right amount of support to Narelle to involve her once more in the activities she enjoyed.
- *Group member death* – Laurie had been going to the singing group for some time when a long-time and well-liked member of the group died. Laurie needed some extra support from the TTR coordinator to understand his peer's death and the change that this meant for him at the group.
- *Group changes* – many groups rely on the efforts and expertise of key group leaders. Where a group leader no longer can come regularly, the group's activities may change. Art group was one of the activities Judy participated in for part of her time at her community group. Interested members worked on their art projects for up to an hour each week before rejoining the larger group. Due to the illness of a close family member, the art group leader's attendance became sporadic. The art group only took place when the leader was present. This often left a hole in Judy's activity schedule. The TTR coordinator spoke to Judy's accommodation staff who pointed out that Judy enjoyed doing certain craft activities independently. These craft materials were provided to the group and stored with the other art equipment. The TTR coordinator then assisted Judy's mentors to prompt her to use these craft materials whenever art was cancelled because the leader did not make it to thegroup.

Structuring monitoring and ongoing support for different people

One important thing to decide when providing ongoing monitoring and support is *how often* you need to make contact and *what kind of contact* (in person, phone) is needed. For example, someone with high support needs and a potentially unstable element in their life is likely to need much more regular monitoring than an individual with very low support needs and a stable life.

> *Mary's declining health and independence*
>
> Mary has a number of health problems that she currently self-manages. She has been attending her community group for almost two years and has a familiar routine during her time there. In the last six months Mary has become more forgetful, and her group-home staff have concerns about advancing dementia. The level of contact and communication between Mary's group-home staff and the community group has been minimal. This means that group-home staff are unaware of any problems Mary may encounter at her community group, and the mentors have no ready way of seeking information or advice from the group home. This situation makes the TTR coordinator's role all the more important.
>
> Of course, the TTR coordinator's main responsibility is how Mary's suspected dementia affects her participation, relationships and support needs at the community group. If she continues to cope well at the group then monitoring by the TTR coordinator can occur monthly or even less frequently. If she begins to struggle at the community group and her support needs increase due to forgetfulness or changing health status, then more frequent monitoring and some support from the TTR coordinator will be necessary. These issues need to be recognised and responded to proactively before they lead to a crisis, hence the need for ongoing monitoring.

8 Monitoring and ongoing support

Establishing a regular drop-in and monitoring routine

Using Mary's situation as an example, let's think about how ongoing monitoring and support could be structured by a TTR coordinator.

Key contacts – establishing and maintaining key contacts is vital. Without well-established contacts the TTR coordinator is unlikely to hear about a problem until it has become a crisis. Each contact needs to know who you are, what role you play in Mary's life, how to reach you, and how often they can expect to see or hear from you. To ensure good quality support, these key contacts should also understand the need to pass on relevant information to the TTR coordinator, such as changes to the person's health, absences from the group, and any other concerns. Key contacts often include:

- group-home manager
- key worker/case manager
- supported employment supervisor/administrator
- family members
- community group coordinator
- key mentors at the community group.

Maintaining contact with the person with disability and these key contacts requires regular monitoring via phone calls and in-person visits to the community group. The type of contact – phone or in person – will rely largely on the persons' support needs *at that time*. Phoning is suitable if there are few support issues, whereas in-person visits are needed for more complex or serious matters. Provide greater support when needed but also encourage independence. Wherever possible, have mentors deliver this support. Offering too much *direct* support can result in the person being unnecessarily dependent on the TTR coordinator.

How often will you phone?

You are aiming for the Goldilocks point between too much and too little contact. Here is a list of possible routines and rationales:

- *Weekly* – this would be sensible if Mary had already experienced some kind of a health dilemma or other personal difficulty that directly affected her participation at the group.

Tracey monitoring a TTR client by phone

- *Fortnightly* – this would be appropriate if there were widespread concerns about Mary, but no current concrete dilemma.
- *Monthly* – when all is running smoothly and there are no immediate concerns, but given that we know that Mary is becoming forgetful then monthly contact would be reasonable.
- *Two-monthly* – this is recommended as the minimum frequency of contact. This lower level would only be sensible if Mary's health and memory improved and were not causing any problem for her or the group.

What will you discuss?

During each phone call the TTR coordinator would discuss:

- how Mary is coping (e.g., issues with self-care or health)
- if she remains an active participant in her usual interests

- whether the mentors' support is available and effective in ensuring that she is engaged in social interaction and activities
- specific issues of concern (e.g., health and forgetfulness) and strategies to deal with those issues.

Phone calls are better than emails or texting because they offer the chance to further build relationships, and to gauge unspoken messages conveyed through tone of voice (e.g., whether the information "Mary forgot her money this week" signifies benign amusement or angry frustration). You can email instead if there is a good reason why phone calls are impractical.

How often will you drop in to the group?

Visiting the group regularly is more time consuming than phone calls, but it is essential because it is the only way to see exactly what is happening and how well the person and the mentors are managing at the group. In addition, your presence is reassuring to the person and the mentors and shows that you are genuinely available for ongoing support. How often to visit is a needs-based issue and will be largely driven by what you know and what you may hear from your key contacts. When you drop in monthly or less often, you probably will also be staying in touch with mentors and/or group leaders by phone between visits. Below is a list of possible scenarios with rationales for visits, also based on Mary's situation:

- *Weekly* – you would only drop in weekly in the event of some kind of crisis, difficulty or other significant concerns while at the group. For example, be if Mary became disengaged from activities she used to enjoy, or those activities were no longer available, the TTR coordinator could work with mentors to introduce new activities (e.g., see Chng et al., 2013, participant 3), implement more effective methods of support, or re-establish old routines.
- *Fortnightly* – this is likely when there is not an immediate crisis, but there are some pressing difficulties that could lead to a crisis without attention.
- *Monthly* – as above, this level of drop-in would be sensible if there are some underlying issues, but they have not yet created any difficulty for the person or the group.

Tracey travelling to a monitoring visit at a community group

- *Two-monthly* – for someone like Mary who may have some underlying issues, but where the situation is stable and presents no difficulty.

The time the TTR coordinator will spend at the group when visiting will vary. A minimum of 15–20 minutes is usually needed – about the time it takes to enjoy a cup of coffee and a chat with the person with long-term disability and/or mentors. Spending that amount of time allows the TTR coordinator to find out so much more than is possible with a fleeting visit while people are busy. If there are issues to discuss, or changes to activities or support to trial, then more time will be needed. When dealing with a (potential) crisis, then an hour or more may be necessary and in rare cases of major problems the TTR coordinator may even need to be present the entire time the person is attending the group.

What will you observe?

During each visit the TTR coordinator observes:

- Does Mary continue to be actively involved in her regular activities at the group? Are there any evident problems (e.g., with self-care or

8 Monitoring and ongoing support

memory) that are interfering with her participation, enjoyment or dignity?
- Are there times when she is socially isolated or appears bored with nothing to do? If so, discuss with mentors what can be done about this. If possible, ask the mentors to try putting the agreed strategy into practice followed by feedback and debriefing (similar to the coaching methods used when providing hands-on support training – see Chapter 7).
- Do mentors continue to offer her reminders and support (enough support but the minimum needed to ensure she is an active participant)?
- You also need to talk with Mary and with her mentors about how things are going from their individual points of view, and whether they see are any issues.
- Finally, it is often useful to stand back and just "hang out" at the group to give interested people the opportunity to approach you with ideas or concerns.

A monitoring visit with Peter who has been volunteering at this charity bookstore for over three years

> *Tip*
>
> Monitoring and ongoing support work best when there is a relationship of trust between the TTR coordinator and key group members, so that an unexpected visit from the coordinator is welcomed as a chance to catch up over a cup of coffee, and not seen as the coordinator checking up on the group. Such relationships are *person-specific* meaning that, as far as possible, the same individual TTR coordinator should always be the one to contact the person, the group and its members.

Communication between the community group and home

Good communication is important to cut down day-to-day problems (see Laura's story later in this chapter). Ideally, this communication should be direct between the community group and home, rather than the TTR coordinator acting as a go-between, especially when the coordinator reaches the monitoring stage and is in contact less often.

The TTR coordinator should support those involved to set up an effective means of direct communication. There are several possible approaches that can be encouraged. A "communication book" that the person takes to and from the group, in which written messages are passed back and forth, is effective, but is a stereotypical disability-service-style approach which singles out the person as different. It would be preferable to normalise such communications by adopting other, less potentially stigmatising approaches, such as:

- Having printed notes/newsletters about future events provided to all group members to take home
- Mentors supporting the person to write down future events at the group in a personal diary (this requires consistent support and monitoring at home and at the group)
- If disability staff provide transport and pick up the person from the group, the staff member could give and receive information via face-

to-face discussion with a mentor or group leader, making sure to involve the person him/herself in these chats
- Encouraging mentors to ring the person's home as needed, and vice-versa.

Annual reviews

Many people who receive a disability service, whether accommodation, day program or employment, have an annual planning system. If this kind of planning is in place, the TTR program should be integrated into these annual reviews. The TTR coordinator should always be invited to the meetings (if this isn't possible, a specific retirement review meeting should take place).

Use these meetings to jointly re-assess how well the TTR program is working for the person with disability and whether change is needed. To support this discussion, the TTR coordinator should bring along summaries of information such as the person's attendance at and participation in the group, progress on key skills (e.g., travel), and any changes at the group and their effect. Discuss future options and check if the person wants to make further changes to their work–life balance, such as cutting down another day at work or even retiring completely.

Annual reviews offer the opportunity for a more formal review. However, arrangements can be changed at any time. If things are not working well or new ideas come up, there should be no need to wait until a scheduled review to plan and take action.

 Cedric (6:10–6:38)
Option for further days at the seniors' group

In this scene Sue explains the future possibilities for Cedric at the seniors' group. Cedric now has a concrete idea of what he'd like to do in the future.

Since the *Transition to retirement* DVD was created, Cedric has dropped another day of work for senior activities. This came about through his annual review process where Cedric, Sue and the TTR coordinator met to discuss the situation and his future possibilities. Cedric said he would like to try craft activities, so he now attends another nearby seniors' activity group on Wednesdays. The coordinator suggested Wednesday so Cedric could also participate in the monthly group outings by his original seniors' group that take place on this day. Not only has Cedric been able to make new friends at his new Wednesday activity group, but he has also increased contact with his existing friends at his first seniors' group.

Returning to work

Even with months of enjoyable membership of a community group, a few individuals decided to exercise their guaranteed right of return (Chapter 2; Appendix B), went back to their previous working hours, and stopped going to their group. This decision was sometimes linked to loss of wages due to reduced work hours, or to other factors. During discussion of this choice, the TTR coordinator should find out if there are other reasons, such as an underlying problem at the group that could be resolved. When a decision to return to pre-TTR working hours is proceeded with, the TTR coordinator should assist with revised arrangements at work and support the person with disability to resume their normal working hours. With a positive TTR experience behind them, the person is likely to be receptive to future TTR involvement when they are ready to restart their journey to retirement.

As well, a careful discussion is needed with community groups, so members understand that the person with disability is leaving for reasons unrelated to the group and its support. Ideally, a positive farewell event (e.g., special morning tea) can be organised so that the person leaves on a positive note.

 Tip

Send a thankyou letter to the community group and maintain contact. In future, another retiring worker with similar interests may

8 Monitoring and ongoing support

> want to join, or the same person may wish to come back to the group if work circumstances change.

As-needed support

Ideally, issues are picked up through regular monitoring *before* they develop into a crisis. However, things can still go wrong. The TTR co-ordinator may then need to increase support to work with all involved to deal with a problem and restructure the situation to try to ensure that the problem does not happen again.

When things go wrong

Laura joined a seniors' social group that goes on outings every two weeks and meets at their local community centre for morning tea on the alternate weeks. Laura needs to bring a different amount of money to her outing days versus her days at the centre. Regardless of the activity, Laura's weekly cost includes money for raffles, bingo, transport, and regular payments for the end-of-year Christmas party. On centre-based days, Laura needs to also bring along a plate of food for a shared meal. The difference on outings is that instead of bringing food, Laura needs money to buy her lunch.

The TTR coordinator arranged with Laura's accommodation staff for Laura to have her money in separate envelopes so that she is not confused as to what she had to pay money for. Things started off smoothly and were all in order.

A few months later, when the TTR coordinator was providing two-monthly drop-in support visits to the group, the social group leader contacted TTR staff distressed. The leader advised that there was a mix up with Laura's money and that Laura had been upset on several of the outings.

It became clear that Laura's money hadn't continued to be given to her in separate envelopes due to a change of staff at the accommodation service. Laura therefore hadn't been contributing to the Christmas party which upset the group members. The TTR coordin-

> ator increased support to Laura and the group. The coordinator also contacted Laura's home and the separate envelope procedure was put into place again by accommodation staff. There have since been no problems with Laura's money.
>
> Accommodation staff explained to the TTR coordinator that Laura was having a few family and personal health concerns lately that were adding to her anxiety. When one of the community group members had mentioned to Laura in a non-threatening manner about her lack of Christmas party payments, this had upset Laura further. When the situation was explained to the community group members they had a better understanding of why the money issues had arisen and could empathise with Laura's current emotional state.

Key lessons from Laura's experience are:

- Minor issues can escalate into serious problems if not dealt with early.
- Mentors and community group members will not necessarily speak up about small concerns, because they "don't want to make a fuss", so the TTR coordinator may need to recognise and respond to potential problems early. This is only possible through regular monitoring.
- The community group leader had a good enough relationship with the TTR coordinator to ring to ask for help.
- The fact that the leader needed to ring may show that monitoring was not frequent enough; otherwise this issue would have been picked up before there was a near crisis.
- The person with long-term disability may not even know that there is a problem, and may lack the social skills to negotiate a solution without support.
- Support for Laura from accommodation staff with the separate envelope system was well established to begin with. These arrangements can break down, so it is important to check with the home regularly to ensure that nothing haschanged.

8 Monitoring and ongoing support

Unintended consequences of a new routine may emerge over time

Sometimes a person's routine of going to their group each week starts off well but over time ongoing monitoring uncovers unforeseen issues that mean that the routine needs adjustment to avoid negative consequences. Colin's situation provides an example of this.

> *Colin enjoys a beer*
>
> After a number of months, Colin had become "one of the boys" at his community group – a lawn bowling club with a licensed bar – and comfortably fitted into the culture by having a few beers after bowling. This resulted in him sometimes becoming tipsy, staying at the club later than usual and missing his bus home, which was a problem for Colin and for others.
>
> Supporting Colin in these circumstances presented a dilemma. He had the right to drink as much as he wished and could afford, but doing so was causing him problems with travel. The TTR coordinator wanted to encourage his interaction at the club, which is a normal part of being a member and socialising with friends. The coordinator helped Colin manage the level of his drinking by talking with him about responsible drinking and the choices open to him. He opted to accept reminders from the club members he drank with to switch to soft drink after an agreed number of beers. Colin was pleased that there were no further problems with missing the bus.
>
> A related issue involved appropriate social behaviour. Colin accepted drinks from others when they paid for a round, but at first did not fully understand that he too was expected to take his turn to pay. In any case, to begin with, he had not brought enough money with him. The TTR coordinator encouraged Colin to buy a round, as this is what friends typically do, and accommodation staff ensured that Colin took extra money to do this.

Concluding thoughts

Establishing stable participation at a community group with good mentor support is not the end of the TTR coordinator's role. Good communication, ongoing monitoring and as-needed support is required indefinitely and offers a number of benefits to the person with long-term disability and the community group. Well-calibrated monitoring means that support is not overly intrusive, but also helps ensure that TTR coordinator picks up issues and responds to them proactively before they develop into more serious problems. However, unexpected problems arise even in well-monitored situations and the TTR coordinator must have the capacity to provide prompt support whenever needed.

Section 3
Broader issues

9
Conclusions

Based on our three-year Transition to Retirement (TTR) research project and several subsequent years of TTR service delivery, we are confident that this approach is *feasible* and *beneficial*, and has enduring positive outcomes for people with disability, mentors and community groups (Stancliffe, Bigby et al., 2013; Wilson et al., 2013). This manual aims to make these benefits more widely available. The various components of the TTR program described in this manual have not been tested individually to see if they each are essential or not, but our research and practice have shown that, as a package, the TTR program is effective in helping people build an inclusive retirement lifestyle.

 Tim Walton (Duration 3:26)
Current success and future challenges

Long-serving CEO of the Australian Foundation for Disability (AFFORD) Tim Walton reflects on the fact that people with disability are living longer. Increasingly they need opportunities to pursue a meaningful third age when they can take up personal interests and give back to their community as volunteers. He notes the remarkable variety of community groups and their willingness to accept new members with disability. Tim points out that the TTR program has

> also been successful for these groups and has helped group members to better understand disability and become even more positive in their attitudes. He presents the challenge that for the TTR program to become available to people with disability nationally it needs funding from government and access to community groups and volunteer organisations throughout Australia.

In this chapter we describe the feasibility, benefits and limitations of the TTR program, and consider alternative approaches to building a retirement lifestyle. We also point out that the TTR approach is not a cheap option and requires a dedicated TTR coordinator position filled by a staff member with diverse and well-developed skills. Finally, we look to the future and discuss how the TTR program could be made available more widely as Australia's National Disability Insurance Scheme begins to be implemented.

Feasibility

When we first discussed the TTR approach, stakeholders mentioned a number of potential attitudinal and practical barriers (Bigby et al., 2011). Overwhelmingly, our experience suggests that either these barriers were less of an issue than stakeholders expected, or that the barriers could be overcome by finding appropriate solutions.

Attitudes

As noted in Chapters 1 and 2, we found that many people with long-term disability had little awareness or understanding of retirement. They were worried that retirement could mean being socially isolated and having nothing to do. Family members and staff had similar concerns (Bigby et al., 2011). The information in this manual and the individual stories depicted in the DVD can help people with long-term disability, their families and staff better understand what retirement could be like, and how to begin to build a satisfying, socially inclusive retirement lifestyle. Our intention is that disability service providers will use this manual as a resource to deliver positive messages

9 Conclusions

about retirement to their clients, families, disability staff and community groups.

Another attitudinal barrier suggested by some, involved community group members being unwilling to accept people with long-term disability into their group. We rarely met such problems. In fact, most groups were welcoming, but were apprehensive about knowing how best to support the person. Our approach of training and supporting group members to become mentors was effective in overcoming these concerns (Chapter 7). Even so, ongoing availability of support as needed from the TTR coordinator was important in assisting mentors to deal with any issues as they arose and before they became major problems (Chapter 8).

Positive attitudes toward including people with disability in community groups are also reflected in contemporary policy and resource materials for community groups for older Australians (Department of Families, Housing, Community Services and Indigenous Affairs, 2013).

Practical barriers

The main areas of practical concern were cost, travel and availability of support. The consistent experience was that costs for the person with disability were low and were not a barrier (see Bigby et al., in press). Many groups charged no fees and for those that did, these costs were low given that most group members had limited income because they were retired, elderly, pensioners or unemployed.

Likewise, the cost of travel to the group was generally low. Participants were recipients of the disability support pension and so could buy a low-cost pension fare when using public transport. Those that used private transport involving a disability service provider or family member usually incurred no cost. Community transport, provided by the community group for example, was very low cost.

Travel is discussed in detail in Chapter 6 and Appendix A. The nature of the individual travel solution varied depending on the availability of transport and the capacity of the person to learn to travel independently. However, in almost every case an effective solution was found through the TTR coordinator working together with the person with disability and key support providers (see Bigby et al., in press). There was only one case where the intermittent availability of transport

Catching the seniors' centre bus

contributed to the discontinuation of membership of a community group. In short, travel is an issue to be dealt with but should not become a barrier.

We described in Chapter 7 how support from trained mentors proved to be viable and effective, with no difficulties experienced in recruiting mentors.

Our experience suggests that disability services tend to be rather disability focused. This often results in them being not well connected to the mainstream community and groups in the local area. A further role for the TTR coordinator is to help build these connections.

Benefits

As well as achieving socially inclusive outcomes, the Transition to Retirement program has other benefits including:

- providing enjoyable activity and companionship for the person with disability, with access to people with similar interests

- taking advantage of the many existing community groups and volunteering opportunities already available in communities, thus avoiding the cost and time needed to set up special new groups for people with long-term disability
- the diversity of mainstream community groups provides an outlet for individuals with very particular interests (e.g., aircraft) which are unlikely to be catered for within disability-specific settings
- low cost for the person with disability
- the person with disability can receive some support from the volunteer mentors from the community group. Once this is well established, the costs of ongoing support of each person with disability are mostly low, because on average little support is needed from the TTR coordinator
- the TTR program gives members of community groups the chance to participate alongside and get to know a person with long-term disability, so strengthening social inclusion and demystifying long-term disability
- the program strengthens the capacity and confidence of community groups to support other people with long-term disability.

Where are they now?

The TTR program has made a *long-term* difference in most participants' lives. To demonstrate this, Table 9.1 shows the current situation of the six people whose stories appear in the DVD. The table illustrates how each person's journey to retirement is different. In the two years since the DVD was made, most people (five of the six individuals) have continued to go to their initial community group *and* have reduced their workdays further by adding new, inclusive retirement activities with the support of the TTR coordinator. Most still work part time. One person retired fully, and one person chose to exercise her right of return and went back to work but later retired.

Table 9.1 Initial and current retirement activities for the people on the DVD

Person	When DVD was made		Two years later	
	Initial retirement activity	Days/week	Continuing and additional retirement activity	Days/week
Graeme	Community plant nursery	1	Community plant nursery	1
			Computer course	1
Cedric	Camden seniors	1	Camden seniors	1
			Seniors' craft and activities group	1
Shirley	Cat protection society	1	NA – returned to work but later retired fully.	NA
Stephen	Coal Loader community garden	1	Coal Loader community garden	1
			Cat protection society	1
Laurie	Seniors' choir	1	Seniors' choir	1
			Volunteer at seniors' centre	1
			Lawn bowling club	1(Sat.)
Judy	Salvation Army community group	1	Salvation Army community group	1
			Have a Chat seniors' group	2
			Fully retired	

9 Conclusions

Judy at her new seniors' group

Limitations

No single approach to developing a retirement lifestyle will suit all individuals or meet all needs. We recognise that the Transition to Retirement program is one of a range of options that individuals will mix and match to suit their needs, preferences and circumstances.

In its current form, our approach may not suit all people with long-term disability. We tested the TTR program with people with mild to moderate intellectual disability and with some people who had other types of disability. Those with more severe disability are likely to need more support, including in some cases support for self-care that mentors may be less willing to offer. The TTR program may not be as effective with people who have higher support needs as community group members may regard them somewhat differently. Therefore, the tasks of finding groups with the potential capacity for inclusion, and of supportive mentors, may be more complex and challenging. Indeed, a doctoral study undertaken in parallel with this project has identified the additional challenges of supporting people with intellectual disability and higher support needs to be included as members of community groups (Craig, 2013).

Our research helped the people who participated to begin their transition to retirement, but few participants retired fully. More work is needed to understand the process of full retirement. In this program, we focused on participation in volunteering and community groups. There are many other retirement-related issues (e.g., retirement income) that people with disability need to learn about. Some relevant disability-specific resources to help with these issues are beginning to be made available (e.g., Australian Red Cross, 2012).

Our participants were all aged 45 years and over. Because of changing health needs or other issues, some people may need to retire before the age of 45. It seems reasonable to expect that the TTR program would be useful for these people as well, but we have no concrete evidence to support this claim. Care would need to be taken that younger individuals who retire did not find themselves involved in age-inappropriate groups or activities.

Similarly, it seems likely that a closely related approach could be used to support younger people with disability to join community groups of people in their own age group. However, we did not specifically test this proposition, so the effectiveness of the approach will need to be investigated in future research and service delivery.

All our work took place in large cities where many but not all suburban areas had well-developed public transport and lots of community groups. These circumstances are different in smaller towns and regional areas. There is Australian evidence that similar approaches can be viable in small regional communities, but there were also challenges because of there being fewer community groups and little or no public transport (ARTD Consultants, 2012).

9 Conclusions

Laurie "barefoot" lawn bowling

Variations and alternative approaches

Alternative approaches are no doubt possible – it may work just as well to introduce a second person with disability to the group; groups that meet on different schedules from weekly meetings may also be viable; having opportunities to socialise with friends with disability is also part of life in retirement.

Our approach has clear benefits but is unlikely on its own to make up a full-time lifestyle. There are many other activities that are enjoyable and appropriate – catching up with former work friends, including at work functions, visiting family, or using small-group community access opportunities for leisure activities such as sport, movies or picnics.

How long does it take to "construct the reality"?

Using existing community groups, rather than funding new retirement groups just for people with disability, makes sense when promoting social inclusion and may well be highly cost-effective over time, although we did not measure cost. Although costs were low for the person with disability, the Transition to Retirement program is not a cheap option despite the fact that ongoing support was mostly provided by unpaid mentors. The TTR staff time needed to provide individualised support to each person varies. It will depend on the group and its members, as well as on the person with disability's social circumstances and abilities. For example, travel training (Chapter 6; Appendix A) can be very time consuming, but only some people need to learn to travel to their group by public transport. Therefore, the figures we report below on the time the TTR coordinator needed to support each of a small subgroup of research participants only provide at best a rough guide to what staff time may be needed.

We found that constructing the reality for each person with disability required between 45 and 170 hours (average = 90 hours) of the TTR coordinator's time. These figures do not count time spent with the person promoting retirement (Chapter 2), but do include support provided when planning with the individual (Chapter 4), finding a suitable group (Chapter 5), establishing a new routine (Chapter 6) and recruiting and training mentors (Chapter 7). These hours only include support and follow up for six months after the person joined a group. The ongoing support described in Chapter 8 is in addition to these hours.

Figure 9.1 illustrates the amount of TTR coordinator support provided to two individuals up to 26 weeks (six months) after they joined their groups. It is clear that a lot of pre-placement support was needed for the weeks before the first visit to the group, which is labelled week 1 in Figure 9.1. The pre-placement support involved planning, locating a suitable group, and beginning to set up a new routine.

Post-placement support involved establishing a new routine, and included mentor recruitment and training, as well as support and monitoring of the person with disability at the group. Participant 1 was given lots of coordinator support with travel training (weeks 3 to 10), but participant 2 was driven to the group by a family member, so

9 Conclusions

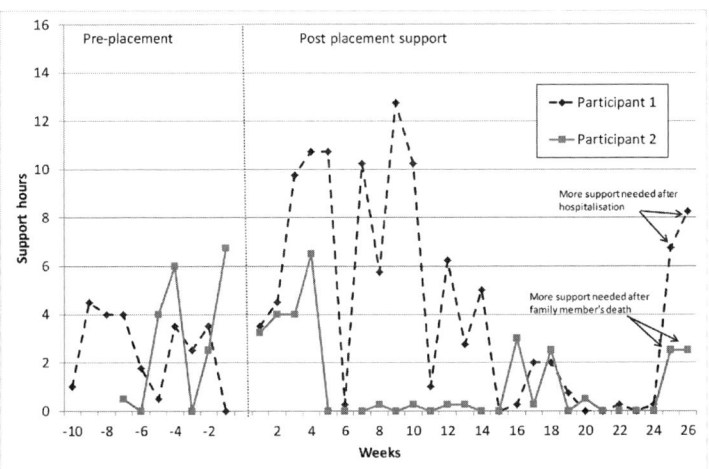

Figure 9.1 Comparison of coordinator hours required during 'constructing the reality' component for two participants. (Figure reprinted from Bigby et al., in press, with permission)

needed no coordinator support with travel. In total, participant 1 received 140 hours of support over the 36 weeks shown in Figure 9.1. Participant 2 was given 50 hours of support over 33 weeks. Both participants received ongoing support and monitoring (Chapter 8) after the 26-week post-placement point, but this is not shown in Figure 9.1.

As can be seen in Figure 9.1, following many hours of coordinator involvement in the first few weeks after joining the group, support hours dropped for both participants. This drop happened after the person had gone to the group for a number of weeks, the mentor training was finished and the new routine was established. It is worth noting that, after weeks of low involvement by the coordinator, both participants had problems that required increased coordinator support for a few weeks (see weeks 24–26 in Figure 9.1). This shows clearly that flexible ongoing support is needed long term in order to help maintain the person's attendance and participation.

Need for a dedicated TTR coordinator position

As just described, the TRR coordinator needs to dedicate many hours of work over many weeks to successfully support *each* individual to plan their transition and to join their community group (Bigby et al., in press). The most intensive support is needed during the planning phase and when establishing a new routine (see Figure 9.1), but indefinite, less intensive ongoing support is also required (Chapter 8). As the coordinator gradually assists more and more people to join groups, there is a cumulative load of ongoing support. In addition, the coordinator must have the capacity to resume intensive support for someone in an established routine, if a major issue arises.

Taken together, all of this information and our consistent experience show that it is essential to have a *dedicated TTR coordinator position*. The TTR role cannot just be added to the duties of an existing disability staff member to be fitted in when time permits. The support that participants need is too intensive for that (e.g., teaching a person to complete a single journey by public transport can take several hours for *each* training session).

For each person with long-term disability, the substantial up-front investment of one-on-one TTR coordinator time is costly, but over time this investment pays off as the person progressively needs less TTR coordinator assistance and can mostly be supported by mentors. Similarly, the TTR coordinator is often the only available individual to provide travel training if the person is going to use public transport. Although very time consuming to begin with, travel training is a good long-term investment, because once the person is independent they no longer need to rely on paid disability staff for transport to the group.

Skilled support

The person in the TTR coordinator position needs a range of high-level skills to carry out this complex role. The person needs to have the following array of skills and knowledge:

- disability expertise, including the capacity to provide training (e.g., travel training) and personal support directly to the person with dis-

9 Conclusions

ability, and the skill to train other people (i.e., mentors) to provide such support
- case-management and person-centred planning skills, including family support
- interpersonal and communication skills to interact effectively and establish ongoing positive relationships with a wide range of individuals and groups
- capacity to inspire people to try unfamiliar options that may be daunting at first, and the capability to negotiate with key individuals and disability service providers to collaborate in order to achieve positive outcomes for the person with disability
- community development skills and the capacity to acquire detailed knowledge of local communities
- problem solving skills, which may include dealing with issues ranging from travel crises to positive behaviour support
- flexibility.

 Dr Nathan Wilson (3:33–4:31)
Need for a TTR coordinator with high-level skills

Nathan Wilson explains that because of the complexity of retirement planning and implementation of the TTR program, a dedicated coordinator position is needed that is filled by someone with well-developed disability-support and case-management skills.

The future: policy, funding and scaling up

The TTR program is fully consistent with the Australian government policy priorities of *active ageing* and social inclusion. However, within the disability sector in Australia, there is currently very limited policy, services and funding dealing with retirement. In such an environment, the challenge is considerable if we are to scale up the Transition to Retirement program to make it widely available to older Australians with long-term disability who want to reduce the amount of work they do or retire.

The transition to retirement program is NDIS ready

In Australia, disability support will be transformed in the coming years as the National Disability Insurance Scheme (NDIS) is rolled out. One important feature of this new approach is individualised planning and funding to access community services and activities.

With the emphasis on a socially inclusive and totally individual approach to building a retirement lifestyle, the TTR program is in tune with the aspirations and funding arrangements of the NDIS. As more people with disability receive NDIS funding, some of them will opt to spend part of this money to purchase support for transitioning from work to retirement.

The following comment from a man involved in the TTR program sums up one important aspect of developing a life beyond work in preparation for retirement.

> The program has helped me a lot to meet other people outside of work in the real world. I have friends also outside of work now.

Readings

This list of readings includes papers arising from our three-year collaborative research project on the Transition to Retirement (TTR) program. Each TTR-related reference is preceded by an asterisk (*). We have also included other key publications related to retirement or support for people with disabilities. Each reading has been cited somewhere in the manual.

ARTD Consultants (2012). *Evaluation of the Australian disability enterprise transition to retirement pilot: final report.* Canberra: Department of Families, Housing, Community Services and Indigenous Affairs. Available online at www.fahcsia.gov.au/our-responsibilities/disability-and-carers/publications-articles/policy-research/transition-to-retirement-pilot-evaluation-report.

Australian Red Cross (2012). *Pathways and possibilities for life after work: a handbook for Australian disability enterprise employees.* Brisbane: Australian Red Cross. Available online at www.redcross.org.au/retirement-handbook.aspx.

* Bigby, C., Wilson, N. J., Balandin, S., & Stancliffe, R. J. (2011). Disconnected expectations: staff, family and supported employee perspectives about retirement. *Journal of Intellectual & Developmental Disability*, 36(3), 167–174, doi: 10.3109/13668250.2011.598852.

* Bigby, C., Wilson, N. J., Stancliffe, R. J., Balandin, S., Craig, D. & Gambin, N. (in press). Transition to retirement: an effective program design to support older

workers with intellectual disability participate individually in community groups. *Journal of Policy and Practice in Intellectual Disabilities*.

* Chng, J. P. L., Stancliffe, R. J., Wilson, N. J., & Anderson, K. (2012). Engagement in retirement: an evaluation of the effect of Active Mentoring on engagement of older adults with intellectual disability in mainstream community groups. *Journal of Intellectual Disability Research*, Epublication on 10 October, doi: 10.1111/j.1365-2788.2012.01625.x.

* Craig, D. (2013). "She's been involved in everything as far as I can see": supporting the active participation of people with intellectual disabilities in community groups. PhD thesis. LaTrobe University, Melbourne.

Department of Families, Housing, Community Services and Indigenous Affairs [Advisory Group: Vision for Sustainable Supported Employment] (2013). *This is our space: ageing with disability*. Canberra: Department of Families, Housing, Community Services and Indigenous Affairs. Available online at www.fahcsia.gov.au/our-responsibilities/disability-and-carers/publications-articles/general/this-is-our-space-ageing-with-disability.

De Vaus, D. Wells, Y., Kendig, H., & Quine, S. (2007). Does gradual retirement have better outcomes than abrupt retirement? Results from an Australian panel study. *Ageing & Society, 27*, 667–82, doi:10.1017/S0144686X07006228

Farris, B. & Stancliffe, R. J. (2001). The co-worker training model: outcomes of an open employment pilot project. *Journal of Intellectual & Developmental Disability, 26*(2), 143–59, doi: 10.1080/13668250020054459.

Mansell, J., Beadle-Brown, J., Ashman, B., & Ockenden, J. (2005). Person-centred active support. Brighton, UK: Pavilion Publishing. For more information go to www.pavpub.com/s-24-learning-disability.aspx?s=1&pagenum&dis=99999.

*Stancliffe, R. J., Bigby, C., Balandin, S., Wilson, N. J., & Craig, D. (2013). Transition to retirement and participation in inclusive community groups using active mentoring: an outcomes evaluation with a matched comparison group. Manuscript submitted for publication.

Stancliffe, R. J., Jones, E., Mansell, J., & Lowe, K. (2008). Active support: a critical review and commentary. *Journal of Intellectual & Developmental Disability, 33*(3), 196–214, doi: 10.1080/13668250802315397.

* Stancliffe, R. J., Wilson, N., Bigby, C., Gambin, N., Balandin, S. & Craig, D. (2013). Self-determination and transition to retirement. *National Gateway to Self-Determination*, April 2013 issue 5, 14–17. Available online at www.aucd.org/docs/publications/nti_selfd_issues/issue5_sm.pdf.

* Wilson, N. J., Bigby, C., Stancliffe, R. J., Balandin, S., Craig, D. & Anderson, K. (in press, accepted 14 March 2013). Mentors' experiences of supporting older adults with intellectual disability to participate in community groups. *Journal of Intellectual & Developmental Disability*.

Readings

* Wilson, N. J., Stancliffe, R. J., Bigby, C., Balandin, S., & Craig, D. (2010). The potential for active mentoring to support the transition into retirement for older adults with a lifelong disability. *Journal of Intellectual & Developmental Disability*, 35(3), 211–14, doi: 10.3109/13668250.2010.481784.
World Health Organization (WHO) (2002). *Active ageing: a policy framework*. Geneva: World Health Organization. Available online at whqlibdoc.who.int/hq/2002/who_nmh_nph_02.8.pdf.

Appendix A
Travel training

This Appendix contains information on:
- choosing to use public transport
- travel planning
- travel training booklet
- travel training, fading support and shadowing
- when things go wrong
- training experienced travellers.

Cedric checking the bus timetable

Using public transport

As discussed in Chapter 6, independent travel by public transport is empowering, as it gives the person the freedom to travel to their community group without relying on someone else. Travelling independently also offers greater access other local activities. Even though travel training is quite time consuming, these important benefits mean that it is often a good investment of the TTR coordinator's time.

> *Graeme (5:11–6:48)*
>
> *Travel training*
>
> The TTR coordinator, Nicolette, teaches Graeme to catch a bus and a train to travel to the community plant nursery. Each session is time consuming because, to begin with, they travel together for the entire trip. Nicolette describes how she made Graeme a travel-training booklet with step-by-step picture instructions (e.g., photos of landmarks). Graeme explains what the photos mean.

There are many factors to consider when deciding whether public transport is viable and is the best available option. These include:

Environmental factors

- Is public transport available between the person's home and the community group at the needed times?
- How far away is the nearest public transport stop?
- What alternative means of transport are available?

Personal factors

- Does the person with long-term disability want to learn to travel independently?
- Do caregivers agree with the idea of independent travel? Are they willing and able to provide practical support, such as reminders about the right time to leave home?

- Are there health, mobility, behavioural, vision or hearing issues that need to be considered?
- Can the person recognise, or learn to recognise, bus or platform numbers? Can the person recognise destination names?
- Does the person have the money skills needed to manage fares, or can supports be provided to help the person with money?
- Can the person communicate enough – verbally or using augmentative tools – to buy a ticket to a specific destination, and to seek help if needed?
- Can the person tell the time? If not, what supports will be put in place to assist?
- Is the person aware of the basics of socially acceptable behaviour while travelling in public?

The match between the person's capacities and the demands of the trip

- Is the complexity of the trip consistent with the person's skills? Trips involving changing buses/trains are more difficult.
- Are the physical demands of the trip within the person's capacity (e.g., walking distances, accessibility)?
- Does the person have the safety skills needed for this journey (e.g., road safety, stranger danger, mobile phone availability and use)?
- Is there an effective backup plan if things go wrong?
- Is the time needed to complete the journey appropriate for the person?

Where the person's capacities do not currently match the requirements of the journey, the travel trainer's task is to teach new skills, simplify the parts of the trip that are currently too difficult, or find sources of support to help the person deal with problems. For example, a person who cannot tell the time can be prompted by others (e.g., mentors) when it is time to leave to catch the bus. Individuals who cannot read the destination sign, can check if they are boarding the right bus by learning to ask the driver "Does this bus go to . . .?" Those with limited speech can learn to show the driver a card with the destination name. If selecting the correct money for the fare is too difficult, a caregiver can assist the person to have the exact money prepared.

These kinds of supports can help people learn to travel independently. Even so, there will be circumstances where environmental or personal factors, or their combination, mean that travel by public transport is not considered viable, and another transport solution needs to be found.

Throughout this Appendix, we provide a detailed analysis of travel training, to cover issues that for may arise for a person with disability who has little or no experience of public transport. For individuals with milder disability and more extensive independent travel experience, readers will need to make a judgement as to how much detail is needed to effectively train a person to travel safely by public transport.

Travel planning

Assuming that independent travel by public transport is an appropriate option for the individual concerned, a crucial first step is planning the journey. The TTR coordinator should:

- Find out what public transport skills and knowledge the person with disability already has. As much as possible, plan the new trip to the community group to build on existing skills.
- Research the public transport options to find out costs, departure times, journey times, safe walking routes, sources of assistance while travelling, where to catch the bus/train and where to get off.
- Travel the route without the person with disability. Note availability of information (signs, posted timetables), landmarks, hazards and potential sources of confusion. For example, if buses that travel to different destinations all pick up from the person's bus stop, then the person needs to select the right bus to catch.
- Plan a feasible, safe journey taking into account relevant health, mobility, behavioural, vision or hearing issues (e.g., accessible buses needed, train station must have an elevator because of problems with stairs).
- If connections to another bus or train are involved, plan the change to be as simple and unhurried as possible. The fastest, most direct route may not necessarily be the easiest.
- As far as possible, plan the trip to fit in with the person's existing life routines. For example, if the person needs to leave home early, then

stopping off for a coffee en route could be built into the trip to avoid arriving at the group too early.
- Take photos of relevant features (e.g., the bus clearly showing the bus number) and landmarks for later use in the travel-training booklet.

The option of using public transport need not be an all-or-nothing choice. Part of the trip can be by public transport and part by other means. For example, no bus was available at a suitable time for Graeme's trip home. Instead he caught the train back to where he would otherwise have caught the bus and waited there to be picked up there by accommodation staff.

Consultation with the person and caregivers

Based on the information just listed, discuss your proposed travel plan with the person, the family and caregivers. Ensure that they are happy with the plan and modify it as needed based on the preferences and options they mention. There can be safety concerns or doubt about the person's perceived travel ability. The TTR coordinator needs to explain the travel plan and the precautions involved. Some disability services require that a risk assessment is carried out – see Jane's story below. A well-prepared travel plan reduces risk where possible, and provides strategies to manage those risks that cannot be eliminated.

Caregivers and family often need to provide support with leaving home on time, as well as with taking the right amount of money for fares and other needed items, so their cooperation in essential.

> *Jane travels to a woodworking group*
>
> Jane wanted to go to a woodworking group for women, but the nearest group was not in her local area. Although Jane was able to catch public transport, she had recently experienced some health issues that left her more dependent on staff for transport with some loss of independent travel skills.
>
> The location of the woodwork group and the time needed to drive Jane there meant that accommodation staff were not able to

> take her to the group. Intensive negotiations were held between Jane, the TTR coordinator and staff at the accommodation service. Jane was keen to attend group and was eager to learn to travel there independently.
>
> The TTR coordinator helped accommodation staff manage their concerns about the risks involved in Jane travelling alone to the woodwork group. Jane received a doctor's clearance and emergency systems were put in place at the accommodation service and woodwork group setting out what to do if Jane did not arrive on time.
>
> After travel training from the TTR coordinator, Jane now travels independently to her woodworking group.

 Tip

Over time, give feedback to family/staff about areas of success and those of concern. They can also have useful training ideas.

One more factor to think about when planning travel training is the logistics for the TTR coordinator. Once the person with disability has travelled to the community group with the coordinator, how will the coordinator return to base without a car? Options include being picked up by a colleague, or staying at the group and working in a spare room, then providing the person with disability with travel training on the return journey by public transport.

Travel-training booklet

 Tip

Provide the person with long-term disability with a personalised travel-training booklet with photos of key points of the journey and its landmarks.

When creating a travel training booklet:

- Make the booklet unobtrusive and small enough to fit into a pocket, purse or bag. Laminating the booklet will make it more long-lasting.
- Use a simple layout with photos and basic words to show the key stages of the journey, step by step and in the correct order. Use photos of the person with disability in the real travel setting.
- If needed, use photos and images of items the person needs to take (e.g., pension card, exact money, drink, lunch).
- Use images of clocks showing the time to leave home or leave the community group. Select digital or analogue clock faces according to the person's preference or to match the available timepieces (e.g., person's watch, clock at the community group).
- Use photos of landmarks to help with navigation (e.g., knowing that the next stop after the landmark is where to get off).
- Highlight important features in photos using arrows, circles or boxes so the person knows where to go and what to look for.
- Show relevant parts of train/bus route maps with the key information highlighted (e.g., destination circled).

Mulgrave Station is the 4th stop

- Provide tips on what to say to the driver (e.g., "Tell the driver you are going to Richmond station").

Transition to retirement

- Highlight emergency contact details (phone numbers and contact person's name for travel trainer, home and community group).

Apart from using the travel-training booklet personally, the person with disability can show it to others when seeking help or information.

Example pages from Graeme's travel training booklet are shown below, including the change from bus to train.

Catch the 677 bus (Westbus) that comes at 8.25 am

Tell the driver you're going to Richmond Station.

The bus will stop at Richmond.

When you hop of the bus, walk towards the Caltex Station.

Cross the road at the first set of lights (Mc Donald's will be in front of you).

Walk to Richmond Station and hop onto the train that's waiting at the station

(North Shore and Western train which departs at 9:10am Richmond Station Platform 2)

140

Fading support and shadowing

You will usually start by travelling with the person for the whole trip. This gives the opportunity to teach the person about good manners while travelling (e.g., queuing, waiting for passengers to get off), how to buy a ticket, where to sit, how to behave while travelling, what to do when approaching your stop, and safety issues.

Tip

Model appropriate behaviour such as safe road crossing and polite behaviour when queuing.

Fading support

For the person to become independent you will need to systematically reduce your support. This can be done in several ways. Use any or all of the methods listed below as individually appropriate.

Withdraw support that is not needed. It may soon become clear that there are parts of the trip that the person understands well and can handle easily. Reduce support for those sections of the trip. If the person knows the way to their local bus stop, meet at the bus stop instead of walking together from home. Likewise, once the person is confident and competent with the first leg of a more complex journey, meet at the place where they need to change buses/trains.

Help the person think and problem solve. When discussing the trip beforehand or when travelling together, encourage independent thinking. Use indirect questions such as "What do you do next?" or "Is there something you have forgotten?" that don't provide prompts within the question as to what to do. Encourage the person to use the travel-training booklet to check information.

Transition to retirement

 Tip

Focus on asking the person questions about the journey rather than explaining what to do.

Fade support. While still travelling together the TTR coordinator can start sitting separately. Sit behind the person so your body language does not give a cue that it is time to get off. Explain beforehand that the person with disability will decide where to get off and the coordinator will follow. This approach gives the person responsibility for key decisions while still providing the safety and reassurance of support nearby. If the person with disability makes a mistake, the TTR coordinator needs to judge when and how to intervene. If the mistake is potentially very dangerous the coordinator should stop the person (e.g., running across a busy multi-lane road). In most cases the coordinator should allow the mistake to happen then help the person to recognise the mistake and work out a solution (see 'When things go wrong' below).

Once this step (sitting separately) has been completed successfully two or three times the coordinator can follow by car or meet the person where they get off.

 Tip

Be consistent when travel training. Walk the same pathways each time, and use transport that follows the same route, at the same time.

Shadowing

Shadowing means observing without the person knowing they are being watched. This gives the person the experience of travelling independently, with the safety of help being available if needed. This approach offers clear evidence of the person's competence and independence to reassure concerned family and staff that the person is safe.

When things go wrong

Don't wait for something to go wrong before thinking about travel problems. Training in how to deal with problems should be part of all travel training. Common issues include:

- missing your bus/train
- bus/train does not arrive because of cancelled services or last-minute timetable changes
- losing your ticket, your money or possessions
- catching the wrong bus/train
- getting off at the wrong stop
- problems with other people (stranger danger, harassment).

Involve the person in discussion about these issues and practise what to do when something goes wrong. This practice can involve:

- Using a mobile phone to seek advice or help.
- Approaching responsible people (e.g., bus drivers, station staff, shopkeepers, police, mentors at the community group) to ask for help. Practise using the emergency contact information in the travel-training booklet when approaching people for help.
- Running a "getting lost" drill where the person deliberately makes a mistake (e.g., catches the wrong bus) then practises how to deal with this situation under supervision.

Make sure the person with disability carries emergency contact information at all time. If a mobile phone is needed, does the person know how to use it to call the right person for advice or help? Is there a support system in place to make certain that the person keeps the phone charged with credit available?

Emergency backup

As well as teaching the person with long-term disability about how to cope with problems, there needs to be an emergency support plan. The plan should ensure that any problems are recognised promptly and that help is available. This means that people at home and at the community group should know what time to expect the person with disability to arrive and what to do if they are late. It also means that the emergency contact information listed in the travel-training booklet must be up to date and the people shown as emergency contacts should be easily contactable.

Training experienced travellers

Regardless of travel ability and whether or not the person with long-term disability already travels the route, we suggest always assisting the person for the first time on a journey. This ensures the person's safety and highlights any areas that need support or refinement of skills. Travelling a known route at a different time can involve new challenges such as an unfamiliar driver or different fellow passengers, as well as minor variations in the route according to time of day.

Observing a confident traveller can lead to the TTR coordinator suggesting other options (e.g., catching the express bus 20 minutes later and sleeping in; walking a quicker, safer or more interesting route).

Setting up a new route for someone who has current travel experience is easier due to the skills and confidence already learnt. Even so, all of the issues mentioned earlier in this Appendix still apply. Ensure the person is a safe and competent traveller on the new route before ceasing support.

 Cedric (5:36–6:08)
Training an experienced traveller

In this scene the TTR coordinator explains how to set up new travel routes with Cedric who already catches a bus and train to work.

Appendix B
Forms

We assume that disability services already have established client information systems, so this Appendix contains only three forms. Each is directly related to the TTR program and to retirement planning. The forms are:

- Retirement Lifestyle Planning form (first retirement planning meeting)
- Retirement Lifestyle Planning form (for annual review meeting)
- Right of Return letter.

To save space these documents have been reformatted by omitting blank sections intended to record discussion and decisions at the meeting.

A note about retirement lifestyle planning

As was explained in Chapter 4, retirement lifestyle planning meetings are run in an informal, conversational way so that the person with disability is comfortable. This approach should inform how you use the planning forms in this Appendix. Consider the questions listed in the planning forms to be only prompts/guidelines for conversation. Not all questions need to be asked or answered in every case. The questions should not be directed to the person one after another, like a rigid questionnaire. Instead, the conversation should flow, with other questions arising naturally from the person with disability's responses. The questions are simply conversation starters to allow you to get to know the person.

Retirement Lifestyle Planning form

(First retirement planning meeting)

| Retiree name: | Date: |

Welcome

Meeting participants

Developing the plan

Past lifestyle
- Where have you worked in the past?
- Tell me about growing up.
- What friends did you have? What things did you do with them?
- Have there been any important events that have affected your life?
- What activities or groups have you been involved with in the past?
- Did you play sport?
- Did you go to church?
- Did you have a pet?
- What things did you like doing at school?
- Did you have any interests or hobbies – things that you enjoyed doing?
- Have you been to any interesting places?

Transition to retirement

Current lifestyle

- Tell us about your family.
- What kind of activities do you do now in your spare time?
- What do you enjoy doing with friends?
- Do you have a particular hobby or collection?
- Do you play sport?
- Do you go to church?
- Are you a member of any clubs or groups?
- Do you have a pet?
- What do you like about where you work now?
- What are you good at?
- What can we do to support you?

Future goals/dreams

- What do you hope for in your life in the future?
- If you dropped a day of work, what kind of activity would you like to do instead of working on that day?
- Would you prefer to join a community group (give examples) or become a volunteer (give examples)?
- What day would you like to drop from work?
- How will dropping a day at work affect your money situation? Do you know that you will receive less pay?

The following issues should also be considered when writing the plan

- Are there any health issues (e.g., epilepsy, medication, diet) that affect your day-to-day activities now?
- Do you need help with self-care (using the toilet, eating or drinking)?
- Do you need support with your mobility (walking)?

- Do you know how to catch a bus or train?
- Is there someone who could drive you to a new activity such as a community group?
- Do you have any worries about transport?
- Do you need support to learn how to travel on a new public transport route (e.g., to a new community group)?
- Are there any social behaviours or communication needs that you need support with?
- Do you have a mobile phone? Can you phone people using your mobile, without help?
- Do you look after your own money?
- How much money can you afford to spend each week on retirement activities?
- Do you know of any other issues that need to be taken into account when choosing an appropriate group?

Identified barriers to retirement

Goals for the next 12 months

Short-term goals (3–6 months)

Transition to retirement

Long-term goals (6–12 months)

Reminder that right of return to original work hours only applies for the first 12 months of being in the TTR program.

Date when right of return is no longer available:_____

Is there anything else you would like to talk about to help your transition to retirement?

Close meeting. Thank you.

Retirement Lifestyle Planning form

(For annual review meeting)

| Retiree Name: | Date: |

Welcome

Meeting participants

Progress since commencement (or last Retirement Lifestyle Plan)

Achievements

Are there any worries or issues that you/staff/family have about your community group?

Transition to retirement

What are the good things that have happened to you since you've joined the TTR program?

Future goals and dreams

- Would you like to drop another day from work? If so, what day and what activity would you like to do?
- Do you want to keep going to your current community group?
- What do you hope for in your life in the future?

Updating the plan

- Are there any new or continuing health issues (e.g., epilepsy, medication, diet) that affect your day-to-day activities now?
- Do you need help with self-care (using the toilet, eating or drinking)?
- Do you need support with your mobility (walking)?
- Do you know how to catch a bus or train?
- Is there someone who could drive you to a new activity such as a community group?
- Do you have any worries about transport?
- Do you need support to learn how to travel on a new public transport route (e.g., to a new community group)?
- Are there any social behaviours or communication needs that you need support with?
- Do you have a mobile phone? Can you phone people using your mobile, without help?
- How much money can you afford to spend each week on new (extra) retirement activities?

- How will dropping another day at work affect your money situation? Do you know that you will receive less pay?

Goals for the next 12 months

Short-term goals (3–6 months)

(Long-term goals (6–12 months)

Reminder that right of return to original work hours only applies for the first 12 months of being in the TTR program.

Date when right of return is no longer available:_____

Is there anything else you would like to talk about to help your transition to retirement?

Close meeting. Thank you.

Right of Return letter

Date _____
Dear _____,

Congratulations for giving the Transition to Retirement program a go. None of us can work forever so trying out some new activities while you cut down your days at work will give you a great opportunity. Hopefully you will meet some new friends and will participate in some activities that you have always wanted to try.

Within the next year, if your involvement in the Transition to Retirement program does not work out and you want to come back to work the same number of days as before, I will guarantee that you can return to your job at Sunrise Industries.

While you participate in this exciting program, if you want to talk to someone about any problems or concerns you may be having, make sure you talk to Martina Fredericks, the Transition to Retirement coordinator. You can phone Martina on (02) 1234 5678 (office) or 0412 345 678 (mobile).

Best wishes,
Stephen Valentine
Chief Executive Officer
Sunrise Industries

About the authors

Roger J. Stancliffe is Professor of Intellectual Disability at the University of Sydney's Centre for Disability Research and Policy. He is a past editor of the *Journal of Intellectual & Developmental Disability* and was awarded the 2011 research prize by the American Association on Intellectual and Developmental Disabilities.

Dr Nathan J. Wilson is a researcher and lecturer at the University of Sydney's Centre for Disability Research and Policy. He has worked in the area of disabilities for 26 years with a background in developmental disability nursing. His research interests are in the areas of intellectual disability, men's health, masculinity, ageing and quality of life for people with profound and multiple disabilities.

Nicolette Gambin has been employed by the Australian Foundation for Disability (AFFORD) for over six years and was appointed as the foundation Transition to Retirement coordinator in 2010. Nicolette has presented at national disability conferences and has co-authored several articles that have been published in national and international journals.

Professor Christine Bigby is the Leader of the Living with Disability Research Group at Latrobe University, Melbourne. She has a published extensively on ageing with a lifelong disability, social inclusion and effectiveness of services for people with an intellectual disability. She is founding editor of *Research and Practice in Intellectual and Developmental Disability*.

Professor Susan Balandin is Director of the Jessie Hetherington Centre for Educational Research at Victoria University of Wellington, New Zealand. She is a Fellow of Speech Pathology Australia and former co-editor of the *Journal of Intellectual & Developmental Disability*. She has held professorial positions in Norway and Australia. Her research interests include communicative interactions and participation of people with lifelong disability.

Index

accessibility issues, 53, 73
accommodation service, 65
active ageing, 15, 31, 127
Active Support, 85
activity adaptations, 89
activity demonstrations, 85, 93
activity sampling, 58
affordability, 62
ageing, 5
annual reviews, 107–108
anxiety, 41
art group, 28
Australian Disability Enterprises (ADEs), vii, xi
Australian Foundation for Disability (AFFORD), ix

bookstore, 48

caregivers, 98
case management, 127
cerebral palsy, 5
change, impact of, 97–99
charity store, 26
charter of rights, 30

choir, 27, 28
coaching of mentors, 86, 89–91
communication, 65, 67, 72, 106
"communication book", 106
community attitudes, 78
community centres, 28
community development, 127
community garden, 52
community groups, 23, 27–28. *See also* mentors
  building relationships with, 31–33
  cost of participation in, 33, 53, 57
  finding, 28
  first contact with, 29, 30–31
  first meeting, 57–58
  informal rules at, 53, 55, 78, 89–91
  key leaders and stakeholders in, 31
  leaving, 108
  location, 33
  long-term participation in, 97
  mapping a new routine for, 70–72
  suitability of, 33–36, 52–55
  timing of, 33
community life, limited experience of, 10

community nursery, 31
companionship, 118
constraints, overcoming of, 67
control, feeling of, 21, 41
conversation supports, 71
creative thinking, 93
crisis, 98, 109–110
cues
  recognising of, 87–88
  offering tangible, 91

dementia, 5, 100
disability
  lifelong, xi
  long-term, xi, 5
disability service staff, 19–20
  education sessions for, 20
  as advocates for people with disability, 29
disability-specific services, 7
disability support pension, 26
Down syndrome, 3, 5

emergency backup, 143
emergency contacts, 140, 143
emergency support plan, 143
employment benefits, 69

flag bearers, 18
forms, 145–153

group culture, 55, 78

health crisis, 97
hospitalisation, 97

incidental social contact, 78
individual retirement planning, 19
informal conversations, 41, 42
information sessions, 19
interests and hobbies, 44

isolation, 71

just enough support, *see* support : as-needed

key contacts, 101
key worker, 43, 98, 101

library, 28
life expectancy, 3

meaningful participation, 16
mentors, 12, 70–72, 78
  as insiders, 78
  as role models, 88
  coaching of, 89–91
  recruiting, 79–80
  rewards for, 94
  training, 80–88
Men's Sheds, 27, 32
mobility allowance, 26
modifying routines, 76
money skills, 135
monitoring, *see* support : ongoing

National Disability Insurance Scheme (NDIS), viii, 128
National Disability Strategy, viii
newsletter, 18, 28
"natural" support, 78

older workers group, 17
opportunities for participation, 86

People First Language, 82
people with long-term disability
  as a fully contributing group member, 70
  as an individual, 33, 51, 58
  attitudes to, 117
  functional skills of, 46

Index

social skills of, 55, 110
specific interest of, 51
stereotypes about, 29
support needs of, 41, 46, 81
person-centred principles, 81, 127
person-centred retirement lifestyle planning, 39
person-specific relationships, 106
personal diary, 106
photo booklet, 63–64
picture schedules, 92
planning, *see* retirement planning
practical activity, 71
"practising" retirement, 47
productivity, 69
public transport, 42, 73, 74
   accessibility and, 134
   options, 73
   viability of, 134–136

reassurance, 63
reflecting on the past, 44
relationship building, 75
restricted social experience, 90
retirement
   as a as a risky proposition , 8
   awareness of, 8, 116–117
   barriers to, 117–118
   disability service staff and, 19–20
   education, 20
   full, 122
   indicators, 20, 22
   promotion of, 15, 17, 19
   re-assessing finances in, 62
   role models, 17
   socially inclusive lifestyle in, 3, 128
   without disability, 7
retirement planning, 3, 8, 42
   forms, 147–153
   meeting, 42–48
   meeting preparation, 39–42

right of return, 21, 108
   letter, 154
risk assessment, 137
routine
   monitoring of, 101
   unintended consequences of a new, 111
routine change, 61–62, 97–99. *See also* modifying routines; support : ongoing
   examples of, 75
   for the community group, 70–72
   for the individual, 62–63
   for work life (the employment service), 68–69
   issues with, 96
   to home life (the accommodation service), 65–67
   to home life (the family), 64–65

support
   as-needed, 85, 87, 88, 109–110
   effective techniques, 91–93
   ongoing, 96–106
   phone call, 101–103
safety skills, 135, 137
school inclusion, 10
seniors' centre, 27
shadowing, 142
sheltered employment, xi
social inclusion, viii, 10, 78, 119, 127
social interaction, 85
social isolation, 10
social skills, 110
socially acceptable behaviour, 135
soup kitchen, 26
staff turnover, 98

thankyou letter, 108
timetable of activities, 84, 86
training, *see also* travel training

Disability Interaction Training, 81–84
  hands-on, 84–86
Transition to Retirement (TTR) coordinator, 29–31, 33, 68, 95–98
  DVD, x, 161–162
Transition to Retirement (TTR) program, viii, 5–7, 47
  annual reviews of, 107
  barriers to, 117–118
  feasibility of, 116–119
  length of, 0–125
  limitations of, 121–122
  planning of, 20
transport needs, 65, 66. *See also* public transport
travel
  as a barrier, 73, 117–118
  backup plan in, 135, 143
  planning, 136–138

travel training, 74, 134
  emergency support plan, 143–144
  fading support and shadowing in, 141–142
  "getting lost" drill, 143
  of experienced travellers, 144
  travel-training booklet, 137, 138–140
  trial visits, 68

vacancies, 69
visits, in-person, 101, 103–105
Volunteer Australia, 25
volunteering, 24–26

wages, loss of, 108
waiting lists, 52
work, returning to, 108. *See also* right of return
working hours, reduction of, 68

Transition to retirement DVD

The *Transition to retirement* DVD has been produced as a series of modules including:

- Six stories following people participating in the Transition to Retirement program. All are long-term employees with the Australian Foundation for Disability (AFFORD) in Sydney. Each story details the experiences of the participant, their families, carers and members of the community and volunteer organisations involved.
- Presentations from the University of Sydney researchers Professor Roger Stancliffe and Dr Nathan Wilson.
- Comments from the then NSW Minister for Disability and Minister for Ageing, Mr Andrew Constance MP, The Chief Executive Officer of AFFORD, Mr Tim Walton and from the key corporate sponsor, The Trust Company.

Transition to retirement

After you insert the DVD, the top menu (shown below) will appear on screen. Navigate to the specific module/story you want to watch (e.g., Cedric) by clicking on the link to that module.

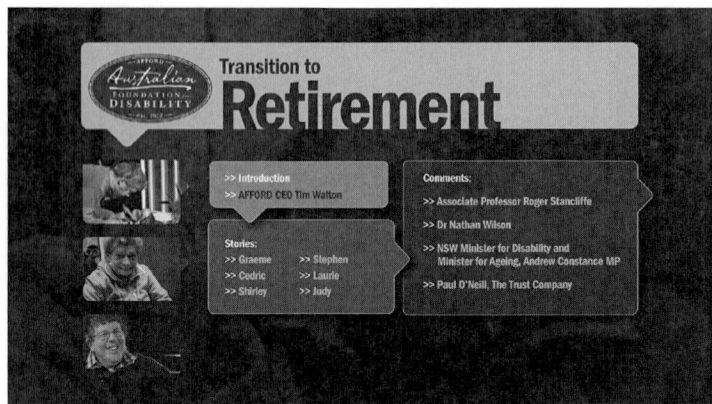